D0527599

GLADIATORS *of the sky*

Their names were:

"*Cat's Eyes*" *Cunningham*, DFC, DSO (two bars)
Jean Maridor, one of the death-or-glory
boys of the Jim Crow Squadron
"*Screwball*" *Beurling*, Canadian
Major Carlo Buscaglia of the Aerosiluratori
Werner Mölders, Lieutenant-Colonel in the
Luftwaffe
Ivan Kojedoub, Soviet air fighter of the
Normandie-Niemen Regiment

and the suicide pilots of "the Divine Wind":
Kamikaze, who flew out to predetermined
death in ceremonial tunic adorned with a
cherry blossom emblem and a silk muffler
waving in the breeze.

*This is a book of the most daring, most
ingenious, most extraordinary fighter pilots of
World War II, regardless of nationality.*

Born To Fly

Georges Blond

A Mayflower Paperback

BORN TO FLY
Georges Blond

Copyright © Georges Blond 1956

First published in Britain by
Souvenir Press Ltd 1956
Published as a Mayflower Paperback 1969

Mayflower Paperbacks are published
by Mayflower Books,
3 Upper James St., London, W.1.
Made and printed in Great Britain by
C. Nicholls & Company Ltd.,
The Philips Park Press, Manchester

CONTENTS

CHAPTER ONE

"CAT'S EYES" CUNNINGHAM

"I THINK all that remains is to bale out," said the chief test pilot.

"I think you're right," replied his colleague.

The aircraft was falling and it was obvious that no manoeuvre or encouragement would keep it in the air. As the patchwork of fields below them grew clearer every second and the sough of the slipstream rose to a scream, the first man eased himself from his seat. His name, which aviation and the cinema have made famous, was Geoffrey de Havilland. The two test pilots baled out and their parachutes opened.

An airman descending by parachute usually does not bother to try and see where he is going to land, contenting himself with pulling if necessary on his liftwebs to alter his direction a little. One rarely sees him, for example, take a small camera out of his pocket and carefully take a photograph of the aircraft from which he has just baled out. This, however, was the sight which met Geoffrey de Havilland's eyes a few hundred feet above the ground on that fine morning in 1938. His companion was photographing the aircraft which was about to crash. He thought that this photo might give useful information about the behaviour of the machine during its fall. The name of the test pilot-parachutist-photographer was John Cunningham.

Now it was April, 1941 and John Cunningham sat at the controls of a Bristol Beaufighter. Above him that night the sky was a milky, icy dome at the peak of which the bright moon seemed like the source of cold. A few miles below, the earth was a vast white circle, in the centre a miniature city from which came a little gleam. London had put out all its fires except one.

Once more the German bombers had returned to rekindle this heart of flame and left – but not all of them, for London now had a very effective defence. But other formations were announced to be on the way. John Cunningham had just heard on his radio the names and numbers locating the enemy in the vast space of darkness; he had entered the network of the ground control interception stations, spaced along the coast. This radio would guide him in the direction of the enemy until they appeared on the screen of his own radar-navigator.

The air battle of Britain at first took place by day. In its first phase which began on the 8th August, 1940, the German offensive was directed against merchant shipping in the harbours from the mouth of the Thames to Portland.

Next the bombers, escorted by fighters, attacked the airfields and factories of southern England. The enemy formations suffered heavy losses but the losses of the British fighter arm were almost as impressive: at the end of August, 495 of its aircraft had been destroyed or put out of service and only 145 remained available. Fortunately for Great Britain the Germans did not know this. The British factories, under the inspired direction of Lord Beaverbrook, made an unprecedented effort and filled the breach.

The next phase of the offensive was directed against London. It culminated on the 15th September, the day 500 German aircraft were engaged by the entire British fighter strength over four counties and the Channel. The minor damage caused in London and its suburbs took an extremely high toll of the Luftwaffe. It became obvious that Great Britain could not be made to capitulate by an aerial offensive. Goering therefore decided to multiply and intensify night bombing (the first raid was carried out on the 7th September against the London docks) and in particular to harass London.

During the following weeks the press and the B.B.C. broadcast that London "could take it" marvellously, almost with a smile. The papers published articles on the ingenious adaptation to life in cellars (the night clubs had built air raid shelters where their clients could lie down and sleep to wait for day: in other words, the end of the raid). Photos appeared showing half-destroyed shops bearing the signs "Business as Usual."

It is true that London bore the brunt of these raids with magnificent courage, but the population suffered a great deal, particularly in the poor quarters which lacked sufficiently deep shelters. From midday queues stood in front of underground station entrances to find a shelter for the following night.

At the beginning of 1941 the bad weather and improvements in the British defence forced the enemy to modify his mode of attack. He began to send little formations of three or four bombers over the capital at sufficient intervals to prolong the air raid alarm for hours. But the British defence began to get organized. Formidable ack-ack barrages were established in the London area. Barrage balloons also constituted a serious obstacle to the German bombers, which never dared to descend below 7,500 feet to drop their loads. Finally and above all, the bombers at great altitude met those adversaries who were to become more and more dangerous to them – the night fighters.

In April, 1941, John Cunningham was 24. This meant that he was considered one of the youngsters in this speciality of night flying which demanded, in addition to the normal qualities of fighter pilots, enormous experience of flying and navigation and a perfect knowledge of terrain. At the altitude at which he patrolled, the night fighter had a view over several hundred miles: or rather, he could imagine it. Here and there, piercing the darkness, he could see the huge luminous cones of the searchlights sweeping the sky. Elsewhere rose sprays of tracer bullets: that was an airfield or some defence point going into action against an attack. Multi-coloured lights would suddenly appear on the ground – an airfield switching on its ground lights for a few moments to allow one of its formations to land. The night fighter had to identify all these lights or intermittent gleams: he had to recognize their nature and sum up the situation in a flash; to have no worries about his navigation while on his way to meet the enemy.

The enemy plane travelled at more than eighty yards a second in a three-dimensional space, either dark or bathed with a milky and deceptive lunar light. The fighter himself flew at a far greater speed. The enemy appeared for a second or at most a few seconds like a fleeting spectre. The problem, to be decided in a split second, was to identify him for certain and not to attack a friendly plane by mistake. Then came the favourable position for the attack and the chase; in fact, the co-ordination of all the qualities of the fighter in conditions infinitely more difficult than those of day combat.

"Night fighting is fascinating work," John Cunningham said one day. "In night combat you are faced with two problems: to outclass the enemy and to conquer the bad weather."

During the greater part of the year the sky is rarely clear above England. Seven times out of ten the night fighters sought, pursued and fought enemy aircraft among rain clouds and sometimes in a storm. These difficulties, added to those we have already mentioned, make one begin to see the difficulties of the task and to imagine the good eyesight that these men had to possess.

These carefully selected night fighters took special precautions to preserve the sharpness of their "cat's eyes." Before taking off or getting ready for ops they remained in very weakly lit rooms, their eyes protected by dark glasses. Certain unit chiefs prescribed for their pilots a diet consisting of concentrated vitamins and carrot juice. The night fighters were subjected to a colossal expenditure of nervous energy and had to be far more temperate than their daylight comrades, for rest taken during the day is incontestably less reposing than night sleep.

"Cat's eyes" was a nickname which Cunningham always modestly disclaimed, insisting that his "eyes" were the aircraft's radar, operated by Jimmy Rawnsley (later Squadron-Leader, D.S.O., D.F.C., D.S.M.).

John Cunningham suddenly saw the bomber ahead of him. Alone and seen in profile in the pale moonlight it looked more like a big fish than a bird – rather like a pike. It was flying level and drawing away to port in the direction of London. Cunningham turned on to its tail and pushed forward his throttle.

This manoeuvre put him in a favourable position because he had the moon behind him. The bomber could not have seen him for it continued to fly in a straight line. Now Cunningham could see his enemy quite clearly. It was a Dornier of the type known as the "flying pencil." "Before I had seen it I was almost petrified with cold. I began to wonder if I should ever feel my hands and feet again, but now the excitement warmed me."

The "flying pencil" went on flying very peacefully and would soon be within range. Cunningham dared not lose sight of it and yet before attacking he wanted to glance at his "office" – this was the name given by fighters to their instrument panel – to see that everything was in order. A rapid glance at the faintly luminous dials. Above all he must not stare at them for he would lose his cat's vision. One of Cunningham's friends told the story that he had once inadvertently touched the switch which lit up a little red lamp. Before he could switch off he was sufficiently dazzled to lose sight of his prey.

Cunningham lowered his eyes for a second. An overall glance at his instruments took no longer. Everything was in order. Once more he scanned the darkness.

The Dornier was still there. It was, in fact, incredibly near. Cunningham just had time to reduce throttle not to run into it. He pressed the button and his eight machine-guns went into action. Almost immediately he saw small flames running along the fuselage and the central escape hatch of the Dornier.

A second later the bomber broke away. Cunningham saw the whole surface of its great wings lit by the moon just ahead of him. Once more he thought that he was going to crash into it. He pulled with all his might on the joystick, just avoided the bomber and lost sight of it.

The Dornier had not replied to his fire. "I wondered if it were playing possum, trying to slip away so as to zoom up on the other side of me and fire, or if it were really badly hit. A moment later I saw it going down below me with a cloud of smoke escaping from it."

John Cunningham dived. Certain bombers when hit,

and even when emitting smoke, sometimes managed to escape, thanks to the skill of their pilot. Cunningham wanted to be quite certain that this one was really falling and not playing any tricks.

The speed of his dive split the lower panel of the Hurricane, letting in the outside air. Cunningham had descended in an incredibly short time from 30,000 to about 3,000 feet. He thought his eardrums would burst, but he could still see the bomber in front of him enveloped in small flames.

At 3,000 feet the Dornier pilot pulled out of the dive and zoomed. Once more Cunningham pulled on his stick and climbed up behind him. He aimed carefully and pressed the firing button. This time the "flying pencil" burst into flames. It stalled, began to spin and fell. Cunningham distinctly saw it crash in the country where it set fire to a thicket.

"I circled round to see if some of the members of the crew had baled out, but suddenly remembering the London balloon barrage, I regained altitude and made for my station."

"My windscreen was covered with oil. This made flying difficult and I had the unpleasant feeling that I had lost parts of my crate. I remembered having seen bits of the German machine flying all around me. There were big holes in my own aircraft, obviously due to debris from the Dornier. I also thought that the engine was revving badly but later examination proved that this was pure imagination on my part. In brief, I landed, made my report, had something to eat and took off once more on a southerly course in the direction of London." John Cunningham's night patrol was not over. Other things were to happen before dawn.

Certain pilots, particularly among the Anglo-Saxons, had boyish faces and did not look more than sixteen years old. Others looked like old sailors. Nearly all of them had a strong chin, and the wide-set eyes of the individual who is quick to take in the events of the outside world. Of all these faces I never found one that surpassed John Cunningham's in intelligence, obvious frankness, reflection and intuition. It is quite certain that when the R.A.F. leaders decided to form night fighter groups they could never have found a more fortunate choice than this airman who had already been a magnificent pilot before the war.

John Cunningham entered aviation, one might say, as soon as came into the world, since he was born in 1917 at Croydon which, in the old days, was London's air terminus. It is not surprising that at Whitgift's School where he studied, one of his first activities was to found a club of young aeroplane model designers. Many of these boys later became lawyers or tradesmen, but not all of them. John never departed from his original idea.

At the age of eighteen he had already reached the first two goals he had set for himself. He was a member of the auxiliary squadron of the County of Middlesex and had procured a job with the de Havilland Aircraft Company. Two years later he was one of their best test pilots. At the beginning of this chapter we have seen how one day, hanging on his parachute, he took a photograph of the aircraft from which he had just baled out with his director.

Called up as a Lieutenant in August, 1939, he was posted to No. 604 squadron, which eventually he commanded. He piloted one of the fighter planes which escorted Mr. Winston Churchill's machine to France in the sombre days of June 1940.

On that bright moonlight night after reporting his victorious combat with the German bomber, John Cunningham took off and flew in a southerly direction towards London.

He glanced at his instrument panel. The altimeter showed 18,000 feet. *Pity I have to climb to 30,000*, thought Cunningham, *the cold is not so unbearable at eighteen.* But he had to climb. He was certain that he would soon hear a message in his headphones reporting the enemy, and that the last words would be "Altitude 30,000 feet" or something in that region. The German bombers usually arrived over England at this height.

John Cunningham not only flew south, climbing steadily,

and waiting for the call on his radio: "I watched the sky."
He watched it not only ahead and to port and starboard of
his aircraft but also turned his head to look over his tail.
In wartime it is as essential for a single seater pilot to look
back as it is to look ahead. Some airmen could carry out
this exercise with surprising ease, screwing their necks
almost to 180°.

Casting a backward glance after passing the 18,000 metre
mark, Cunningham spotted an aircraft. It was a Heinkel.
He identified it immediately over his shoulder. The German
aircraft was following him quietly, close behind. How long
had it been there? One can guess by John Cunningham's
account that he found this a bit tricky. Did the Heinkel
intend to attack first or did he hope to reach London in
this way without being seen? He did not wait to ask
himself any questions. He had already pushed the throttle
forward, made his manoeuvres, and now he was on the
bomber's tail.

The Heinkel was the first to open fire at 350 yards.
Cunningham saw the tracer bullets, but they sped above
him. He drew closer in zig-zags and fired in turn. There
was no result. On an upward climbing turn he saw that
none of his shots had hit the target. The Heinkel continued
on its way, little impressed, and opened fire again. Once
more Cunningham saw the curve of the tracers coming at
him from two angles. He attacked the Heinkel in a
shallow dive, firing with all his eight machine-guns.

This time he realized that he had hit the target. From
the left of the Heinkel a parachute unfolded and then a
second. The two white domes of the parachutes looked like
strange little planets in the moonlight.

Far below them, slightly to the east, Cunningham could
see the outlines of the coast, clearly defined, with an enormous pale petrified fringe: the sea. Slowly losing altitude,
the bomber made for the sea, but the pilot and the third
gunner had not yet jumped.

Cunningham returned to the Heinkel and attacked two
or three times. The last two occupants had still not baled
out and perhaps they were dead. The bomber lost height
more rapidly: "A trail of white smoke was coming from

one of its engines but the machine was still not on fire. I fired another seven bursts until I had no ammunition left. The two engines were smoking and the bomber was still losing height. I followed it for a long time and then lost sight of it at the moment it flew over a black dot on the sea."

The black dot was a ship, the crew of which on the following day confirmed the crash of the Heinkel which was added to the score of the night fighter.

The B.B.C. told the story of this fight in 1941, during one of the broadcasts destined to solace the sorely tried British public. Naturally the pilot was not named. At a later date the action was attributed to John Cunningham. It corresponds to the citation he received on the 23rd April, 1941, which earned him the D.S.O. (he had won the D.F.C. four months earlier). By that date Cunningham had destroyed in night combat at least ten enemy aircraft and damaged several others. The citation ended with the words: "His courage and skill are an example to all of us."

The British night fighters became more active and better organized as the weeks passed. Formations of several fighters, guided from the ground, took off to meet the enemy. As soon as the latter came in sight the leader of the formation gave his orders and the German bombers found themselves attacked from several directions.

Wing Commander John Cunningham was one of these leaders. He displayed a tactical intelligence which was no way inferior to his individual skill. Under his orders his unit gained a number of victories. On the 24th July, 1942, he was given a bar to his D.S.O. as a reward for his efficiency as a unit leader and for having personally shot down sixteen enemy aircraft, all save one during night combat.

One of these opponents was shot down without Cunningham having to fire a single bullet. It was at the end of an engagement and the Wing Commander had used up all his ammunition. He dived on the German bomber with such determination that the pilot plunged towards the

15

ground, pursued by Cunningham who hurtled down behind him like a meteor. The German pilot could not pull out in time and his machine crashed.

For a time he was transferred to Staff. The R.A.F. leaders who were constantly striving to perfect their night fighting organization did not wish to deprive themselves of the collaboration of the greatest expert in this specialized task.

Technical progress, particularly in the field of radar allowed more and more precise guiding of the fighters in the darkness. On arriving at a sufficiently close distance from the enemy, the navigator saw the outline of a four-leafed clover appear on his radar screen. When the latter were exactly equal the fighter knew that he was on his exact course and that he only had to continue until he could see the enemy for himself. Some months later the silhouette of the enemy aircraft was exactly reproduced on the screen.

Ground radar was also perfected. As they moved about the sky the pilots were "taken in charge" by one ground station after the other. These listening posts informed them constantly of the position and the course of the enemy and reported the dangers existing in the sector as, for example, the barrage balloons. Hertzian guiding apparatus of the Lorentz type allowed the pilots to take off and land blind.

All these improvements facilitated and at the same time complicated the task of the night fighter. But at the moment of attacking the enemy nothing could replace the spirit of decision, the manoeuvring skill and the cat's eyes.

When in early 1943 Cunningham left his staff job to take over No. 85 squadron, flying de Havilland Mosquito two-seater night fighters, he proved that he had lost none of these qualities. On the 2nd January, 1944, he shot down his twentieth enemy aircraft. On the 1st March, he received a second bar to his D.S.O. with the following citation: "A magnificent leader whose exceptional skill and wide knowledge of all the aspects of night flight have contributed to a large degree to the exceptional efficiency of his unit which has destroyed a great number of enemy aircraft. His inflexible determination and his rigorous regard for duty set an example which is beyond all praise."

The efficiency of pilots with cat's eyes had already borne fruit. Even at night the German bombers risked their noses more and more rarely in the British sky. The night had become as dangerous as broad daylight. Detected before they crossed the coast, pursued, ruthlessly tracked down, they suddenly saw themselves surrounded by executioners and they were often attacked and brought down before they had time to see anything.

Moreover the chances of the Third Reich weighed less and less heavily in the scales of war. Very few bombers took off from the German and occupied territory bases. These bases were now used by German night fighters which had all their work cut out to defend Berlin and the vital sectors of their country. We know that they, too, displayed great courage and skill. But the British night fighters had been the pioneers, had waged the struggle in the darkness and in the most difficult conditions at a period when they had to call upon all their exceptional qualities as pilots and fighting men.

John Cunningham was to continue his famous career after the war, becoming the holder of the altitude record, which he carried to 59,446 feet (18,071 metres) in a de Havilland Vampire. Since 1946, he has been de Havilland's chief test pilot. When I think that this magnificent flying man continues to risk his life, I must confess that I long for the robot test pilot. But John Cunningham, I am sure, does not hold this opinion.

CHAPTER TWO

JEAN MARIDOR
OF THE JIM CROW SQUADRON

IT was August, 1941, but it could quite easily have been November on that sandy, sinister, treeless shore of Wales. The wind was blowing almost a hurricane and a high sea was running. A Beaufort bomber appeared almost touching the waves, swaying and obviously badly damaged. A few seconds later it was seen to fall into the sea and sink. It had doubtless tried to reach Valley airfield which was only half a mile away.

Airmen from the station and local country folk had gathered on the windy sand-swept shore, looking at some small black dots, which were men trying desperately to swim ashore: the bomber crew plus the six men of a life-boat which had just turned back. Other men went into the water to try and swim to the aid of the shipwrecked airmen.

"They're mad!" said those on the shore. "They'll be drowned too."

Other flying personnel and villagers hurried to the scene. A roar was heard above the beach and a Spitfire sped across the sky. They saw it descend almost to wave-top, swoop over these hardly visible dots on the sea, regain altitude and return. Three times it flew over the struggling men, several of whom had already disappeared. On the fourth run something fell from the Spitfire.

"He's dropped a dinghy," cried the men from the airfield. "No – it's no good."

Carried away by the speed of the aircraft and the wind, the dinghy fell far from the men in the water – several hundred yards away, in fact. The Spitfire had nearly hit the waves. It regained height once more and continued to circle. But, in his despair, the pilot could do nothing. One by one the swimmers were giving up the unequal fight. The Spitfire set its course for the beach again and several of the airmen recognized its markings.

"That's Flight Commander Mouchotte," said one of them.

René Mouchotte had won his first air victory a few days before. He had been a Flight Commander since the 5th August, which meant that the Air Ministry had not waited for this first kill to give the young French Lieutenant his own command – a British flight, a precedent which was considered quite sensational. The R.A.F. had already recognized in him something more than the perfect, skilful and cool-headed pilot. Fighter Command had discerned his intelligence, a talent for organization, an amiable firmness, understanding, teaching gifts; in fact, all the qualities of a leader. We know that René Mouchotte was later given command of a British squadron and then of the "Alsace" group, at the head of which he was killed in air combat. The publication of his notebooks, which have been widely read, did a lot to make the memory of this ace pilot famous. Because there is little to add to this portrait of René Mouchotte – nor to that of Clostermann, his subordinate and pupil before in turn becoming a fighter virtuoso and a French ace of aces – I have decided to give here a picture of another French pilot who was among the airmen who rushed up from Valley on that 30th August, 1941 – Jean Maridor.

The name of this little stocky man with the wide-awake eyes and the streamlined profile is probably less famous in France than it was in Great Britain. According to all the testimonies of his comrades he spoke far more willingly of others than of himself and as far as I know he did not leave behind any memoirs. He lived only for action: to fly and to fight. However, the short life of Jean Maridor, a grocer's son and former hairdresser who became a Captain in the R.A.F. with a score of fifteen victories, in addition to twenty-five ships sunk, would make a very remarkable film script.

Parents who have excessively shy or acutely sensitive children are often quite wrong to worry. That is to say, they would be far more worried if they could foresee that their timid little fledgling would one day become a daredevil. As a baby, Jean Maridor (his baptismal name was

Jean-Marie and he was born at Le Havre in 1920) wept every time he saw a strange face. At the age of three the whistle of a tug would bring on a fit of hysteria. But how mysterious is childhood! A few months later M. and Mme. Maridor could not resist going to an aviation meeting at Bléville aerodrome near Le Havre. Having no one with whom they could leave their small boy, they took him along with them.

"We shall have to see," said his mother, "if it really upsets him too much I shall have to take him home."

But as soon as the small boy saw the aircraft and heard the thunder of the engines he jumped up and down with excitement. From that moment he became a normal, calm and very reasonable child. He was even studious, docile and attentive at his primary school.

"Why don't you make a teacher of him?" the Principal said to M. Maridor when Jean received his School Certificate.

The Maridors kept a small grocery. If they made their son a teacher it would be a step up the ladder. Jean was sent to High School. He immediately lost all interest in his studies. His mind and heart were possessed by aircraft. He built models of them in meccano. True, most young boys do the same, but few of them, as soon as class is over, run to the neighbouring airfield to help polish the machines. That is what Jean Maridor did at the age of thirteen. The owners of private aircraft laughed and said to him: "Well done, sonny; here's something for you." But Jean refused to take any money.

"No, thanks," he replied. "You can take me up one day when you've got room."

In this way he began to fly occasionally as a passenger. His marks at High School grew more and more lamentable.

"I've had enough of this game," his father told him one day. "You must leave school and knuckle down to a job. What do you want to be?"

Jean thought perhaps that it was too early to say a pilot, so he replied: "I don't know."

"Very well, then," said M. Maridor. "I'm going to apprentice you to our neighbour."

The neighbour was a hairdresser. For three years Jean cut hair and lathered beards with very little conviction. He continued to spend all his spare time at the airfield. During the day, as soon as an aircraft flew over, he left his client and hurried outside the shop to watch it. The proprietor was not impressed.

"Well, are you going to settle down and come to your senses or not?" his father demanded in 1936.

"Yes," said Jean. "I want to be a pilot. A test pilot."

Maridor was neither a fool nor a bad father.

"All right," he said. "Since that seems to be the only thing that interests you, go ahead. But be a good one. I'll give you all the help I can. Let's go and find out some information from the Flying Club."

To become a civil pilot and to earn your living in this profession, it was absolutely essential to possess a military pilot's certificate. The only way Jean Maridor could enrol in the Armée de l'Air was to attend the N.C.O. pilots' school at Istres.

"There's an entrance examination," said the chief pilot at the Flying Club. "The level is almost that of a High School passing-out certificate."

"Do you want to go on with your studies?" M. Maridor asked his son.

"Yes."

"Do you want to go back to High School or enter the Lycée? I will pay for your studies and your keep."

"No," said Jean. "I'll take correspondence courses and carry on at the barber's shop."

He worked out his plan. It is curious to see how determination brings out the resources of the individual; from that day Jean Maridor became a model pupil and a good barber's assistant. During the day he was in his shop and at night he pored over his note-books.

Between these two occupations Jean Maridor found time to visit the aerodrome occasionally and to obtain his civil pilot's certificate. He got his "B" certificate at the age of sixteen and the "A" certificate at eighteen. His first instructor carried out a certain number of aerobatics to see whether the young enthusiast could be put off as soon as he was given something a little less pedestrian than straight flying. Jean never batted an eyelid and the instructor went on flinging the machine about the sky. When he finally landed he himself felt quite weary.

"How did you like it?" he asked his pupil.

Jean did not seem eager to leave the machine. "It was marvellous," he said. "If you were really decent you'd take me up and do it again."

As soon as he took hold of the controls this youth, who had been an almost pathologically nervous baby, showed the ease and confidence of people who are born for flying. He passed his "A" certificate in appalling weather, shivering in an open cockpit but completing his circuit (Le Havre-Dieppe-Berck-Abbeville-Le Havre with landings and take-offs), and carrying out his manoeuvres with perfect control. He could hardly foresee that one day he would become a specialist in bad weather flying.

At the 1939 May session he did brilliantly in the exam for the Istres School. He signed on for five years in the Armée de l'Air and received passing-out orders on the 1st September, 1939. He was posted to the Angers School, a subsidiary of Istres. Among the pupil pilots on his course he was the only one without a degree. This did not prevent him from being top in flying and theory.

In March, 1940, he was sent to Etampes where they said to him: "Corporal Pilot Maridor, you're a lucky man. You'll soon be flying a Dewoitine 520."

This was the only French aircraft capable of fighting on even terms with the Messerschmitt 109. The first of this type were put into service on the 15th May, 1940. Jean Maridor was given his in June a few days before the Armistice. Forty-eight hours later he received the order to destroy it. His unit had retired to the south-west of France and the Germans continued to advance.

Jean Maridor left Biarritz with five of his comrades on board a fishing boat bound for England. To try to reach England in this vessel was ludicrous, but in 1940, one out of every four ships on the high seas was British. Forty-eight hours after setting sail he and his companions were picked up by a British merchantman.

"At the end of the first year of the war the R.A.F. found itself faced with a difficult but romantic problem." Hector Bolitho wrote in his book *Combat Report*. "The air force had to absorb hundreds of European pilots who had come to Great Britain after their own countries had fallen to the invaders. During the first months the Poles and the Czechs had crossed Europe to join what had originally been an essentially British service. Then arrived Norwegians, Dutch, Danish and French pilots who had escaped to carry on the struggle. ... " The arrival of these pilots was a nightmare. It was not easy for the R.A.F. to absorb them with their various languages. Numerous wing and squadron commanders found themselves in command of pilots who did not speak a word of English.

Needless to say, the Frenchmen were obliged to correct the deficiency very quickly or the most terrible misunderstandings would have ensued. Next, those arrivals who were fully trained, and some of them even magnificent pilots, had to fly British machines and to learn the organization, regulations, tactics and the unspoken but imperative tradition of that "essentially British arm," the R.A.F. For Corporal Jean Maridor, who had hardly left Flying School and had never fought, the assimilation of all this knowledge must have been a formidable and not particularly romantic task.

The French who had come to England to continue the struggle were welcomed like brothers the moment they touched British soil – whether in Great Britain or at Gibraltar where René Mouchotte and other French pilots had flown over from North Africa – but the R.A.F. immediately examined each particular case with that extreme circumspection always shown in Great Britain to anyone who is not British by origin. It was not sufficient to have a rank and to produce certificates – most of those who arrived had not had the time to collect all their papers – or of saying: "I was this and I did that." They had to furnish proofs in plenty.

Jean Maridor, therefore, began to learn English, followed by a long course of instruction in the R.A.F. He had to get used to the boorish humour of sergeants entrusted with inculcating in all these foreigners – pilots or not – a knowledge of British military regulations down to the smallest detail. Various training centres helped him to relearn in English according to the British methods and customs everything he had already learnt in France: the theory of flying, navigation and radio transmission. At last he was given permission once more to climb into the cockpit of an aircraft.

At St. Atham near Cardiff, and then at Odiham near Salisbury, he flew aircraft that were slower and less difficult to pilot than those he had flown in France and infinitely less interesting than the Dewoitine 520 which he had hardly had time to handle. They were, however, different in certain mechanical respects, necessitating the re-education of certain reflexes: for example, the throttle functioned in the opposite direction, so that for take-off instead of pulling it back it had to be pushed forward. This simple detail caused a lot of accidents and even deaths among pilots from the Continent. At the Sutton Bridge Centre, where he was eventually sent, the average of fatal accidents was one a day. Here the foreign pilots were tried out on Hurricanes. The Hurricane had a maximum speed of 335 m.p.h. and its instrument panel was very complicated. The pilot had to manoeuvre fourteen controls or switches before take-off and any omission could cause a fatal accident. Jean Maridor, like the rest of his comrades, patiently learned the mnemonic phrases which they repeated as soon as they got into the pilot's seat.

After individual instruction on the firing range came formation flying. In fighter squadrons close formation was the golden rule in the R.A.F. and with certain units it was an almost maniacal obsession; on occasions their wing tips were almost touching. It is true that this discipline formed an effective defence measure in those combats when they had to face a superior number of fighters during the Battle of Britain, and later on the Continent.

When the R.A.F. considered that the French Corporal had sufficiently well assimilated his teaching and was fit to fly in a British fighter group, he was promoted to

Sergeant-Pilot and posted to No. 615 Squadron at Valley.

Naturally during this long apprenticeship he had explored Great Britain as much as a twenty-year-old boy, who was not very rich and rather lonely in this country which was so close to France and yet so exotic in the eyes of the French, could do during the first year of the war: little brick towns that looked all alike in the middle of a green countryside, seaside resorts where young boys and girls played tennis a few yards away from the concrete pill-boxes and barbed wire of invasion defences; the big industrial towns with their smoky suburbs and the pubs where one drank beer instead of wine. . . .

On several occasions he went to London. It is highly probable that in common with many other pilots he was given permission to take a look at the famous operations room, the brain of the R.A.F. buried two hundred feet below the ground, where all the information on the enemy formations flying towards England was centralized and from where orders were dispatched to the fighter squadrons. Here on an enormous table-map of England, young girls armed with rakes moved little symbols representing enemy aircraft while officers on a dais, aware at each second of the position of all the British squadrons, telephoned to the individual stations.

When Jean Maridor arrived at Valley the morale of the pilots was not good. Not that they were depressed or reluctant to fight; on the contrary, they were furious at not being able to fight soon enough. Since his arrival No. 615 Squadron, known as the Churchill Squadron, which had become famous during the air battles over London, had been detailed to escort convoys in the Irish Sea. It was a tiresome and thankless job. Few brushes with the enemy, few encounters with the chance of winning brilliant victories, while the pilots of other squadrons increased their score. The rumour was current that the squadron would spend the whole winter at Valley. René Mouchotte wrote to London that he would volunteer for anything, even to fight in Russia. Jean Maridor asked him to convey to Fighter Command that he would volunteer in precisely the same conditions. On the 6th September, the order came through that the unit was to be transferred to the "advanced base" of Manston.

Manston is on the south coast of England near Ramsgate. When the pilots of No. 615 Squadron, after crossing the whole breadth of England in their Hurricanes, arrived above Manston airfield they saw the traces of German bombs. The pilots who were there also explained to them the meaning of the little mounds which surrounded the airfield.

"The airfield has been mined in case of invasion. We can blow the lot up in a second. Now as regards our job – attacking enemy shipping. . . . "

"Sounds more fun than escorting convoys," said the new arrivals.

"Yes and no. We're within range of coastal batteries here. From Cape Gris-Nez Jerry can see us through his telescopes. So there's no question of taking off and circling round to get into formation. As soon as you're airborne you have to slip in between the trees and hedge-hop seawards."

No. 615 Squadron had just relieved No. 242 Squadron. René Mouchotte and Jean Maridor found several Frenchmen among them: Capitaine Dupérier, who later was to command brilliantly the "Ile-de-France" Group, and Lieutenant de Vaisseau de Scitivaux, later to be missing in combat on the 10th April, 1942.

Dupérier and Scitivaux, as well as Sous-Lieutenant de Labouchère and two British pilots, were posted to No. 615 Squadron to show the newcomers the ropes and remained at Manston while No. 242 went to Valley.

Every day or every other day or several times a day the Hurricanes of No. 615 Squadron took off alone or accompanied the bombers. Without gaining height they slipped between the rows of trees towards the sea, hedge-hopping over the little defence works on the beaches. They then flew over the sea at altitude zero; that is to say, skimming the waves so as not to be detected by possible German radar.

The weather was nearly always favourable for their

particular task; in other words abominable, with low clouds and rain. At two or three miles from the reported enemy convoy the formation climbed to about 1,800 feet and then dived on its prey.

The German freighters sailed close in to the French, Belgian or Dutch shore, and they were nearly always well provided with anti-aircraft guns and escorted by flak sloops which spat sprays of fire. In principle the Hurricanes had to put the flak ships out of action while the bombers attacked the cargo boats. These attacks were murderous for the ships. Despite their own defences and the flak ship guns each convoy lost several units.

The attacks, however, were almost as murderous for No. 615. The bombers came back riddled like colanders or did not return at all. The Hurricane pilots considered that they were lucky to get off scot free when the operation went off favourably, that is to say, without intervention from the Messerschmitts. As soon as the Me's arrived the attackers of the convoy became a prey in turn. The German fighters dived on them. The engine power of the Hurricanes did not allow them to gain sufficient altitude from sea level to engage in combat. Their only defence was to flee at full speed in zig-zags as close as possible to the water. This flight was a terrible physical and nervous ordeal. Hurricane pilots attacked in these conditions had very slim chances of survival.

The French who knew Jean Maridor when he joined No. 615 Squadron described him as a cheerful, expansive youth, always impatient to be in action. He took his part in the destruction of several German ships but he does not seem to have been particularly outstanding during the first few months. His hour was yet to come.

A rumour was rife among the French pilots of all the stations that the Air Ministry had decided to form an exclusively or nearly exclusively French fighter squadron. On the 29th October, the list of the pilots transferred to this new unit, No. 340 Squadron or "Ile-de-France" Group, was posted on the notice-board at Manston. It contained the names of Dupérier, Scitivaux, Mouchotte and Labouchère, who were to report on the 7th November to Turnhouse near Edinburgh. Maridor's name was not on the list.

He was posted shortly after this to the British No. 91 Squadron, known as the "Jim Crow Squadron." The mission of this unit, which replaced No. 615, was still to keep the enemy-occupied coast under observation, to control all the channel ports and to attack every aircraft and any naval vessel in this sector. Facts were to show that Jean Maridor had found exactly the type of fighting which suited him. Here is a glimpse into one of his missions.

The operational orders ran: "Attack on the seaplane base at Ostend and eventually any enemy shipping lying off this port." Jean Maridor left with a British pilot but a few minutes after take-off the latter had to turn back because of some mechanical defect. Maridor continued on his own. He was now flying a Spitfire.

The wind was blowing a gale. At moments the low clouds almost grazed the white horses. Maridor, like the rest of his friends from the Jim Crow Squadron, considered the weather ideal. For an unexpected arrival at the enemy ports anything was better than a clear sky and good visibility.

The first difficulty consisted in checking his navigation so as not to crash into the enemy coast, but Maridor had learned to navigate in the worst possible conditions and moreover possessed a kind of bird sense with which he practically divined the proximity of land. He now felt that it was not far off and the next moment saw the silhouette of a little cargo vessel to his left not many feet below him. He banked to the right and described a semi-circle, gaining a little height, and side-slipped down. The cargo vessel was not alone. Three other larger ones were steaming ahead of it between two rows of flak ships. Maridor followed the line of the freighters in enfilade at mast level. He had time to see the men running to their guns, others flinging themselves on their bellies on the decks, while his shells blasted holes in the plates. He was over the third vessel before the flak ships opened with an impressive volume of fire. But he knew that his Spitfire with its supercharger in action at low altitude was a difficult object to hit and he was already in the clouds.

Returning to the small convoy after making a half-circle he saw that jets of white steam were spurting from one of the ships. He dived once more on this victim with all his weapons blazing, passing beneath an archway of tracer bullets from the flak ships, and then zoomed back into the clouds. He returned for a third run in on the convoy, this time approaching it from the beam. The second vessel, enveloped in steam, seemed to have stopped its engines and to be listing, its crew were busy lowering a lifeboat.

Jean Maridor saw all this with the pilot's instantaneous global vision which he possessed to a very acute degree, without forgetting to manoeuvre to avoid the flak ship tracers. He wondered whether he should not make one more attack on the convoy and felt an enormous urge to attack one of the flak ships as he had already done on several preceding missions. He dismissed this idea, however, because to be really effective this particular type of attack required the co-operation of several attackers. In addition, the escort's radio was undoubtedly signalling furiously and it was better not to remain there on his own for a squadron of Messerschmitts to arrive. The worst-hit ship would probably sink or have to be abandoned; moreover, his orders were to attack the Ostend seaplane base. Maridor set his course by compass for Ostend, hoping that all the evolutions necessitated by the attack on the convoy had not thrown him too much off course.

The houses of Ostend appeared like sombre blocks looming to the sky. It was now raining hard. He saw the long beach and the flak batteries on the shore, but no flashes left their muzzles. The seaplane base was a stretch of water behind the port.

Maridor sped like a whirlwind across the grey water of the basins, upon which the ships seemed to be glued like models on cardboard. He arrived over the base. It was deserted. Not an aircraft to be seen. Suddenly he spotted a strange camouflage at the water's edge. Without hesitation he thrust the joy stick forward, firing as he dived. He felt the blast of an explosion beneath his aircraft and saw a great glow of yellow flames lighting up the cloudy damp mass ahead of him. It must have been a petrol dump or a gasometer, he decided.

Now he only had to return seawards by diving through the mist. Maridor realized that he was about to cross the coast again when he distinguished ahead of him hundreds of black mushrooms of flak. Below this a wall of flashes. A few seconds later the wall was behind him. A few more black puffs round his aircraft and then nothing.

He descended once more to altitude zero. Other fighter pilots, no less courageous than himself, only felt at ease in a fight at high altitudes. Some of them had moved heaven and earth not to be transferred to or to remain in this Jim Crow Squadron, finding hedge-hopping warfare over the water too unrewarding or too difficult. But Jean Maridor loved this type of warfare and flying. He skimmed above the foam with the delight of a gull, happy at feeling swift and free, close to the heavy green masses in the violence of the elements.

He thought, too, with satisfaction that in less than an hour – the time to land and hand in his report – he would be sitting drinking a pint of beer in the light and warmth of the Officers' Mess, for Sergeant Maridor had been promoted to Lieutenant. But in this squadron the atmosphere of the Officers' Mess was as simple and cordial as a boy like Jean Maridor could have wished for. They were a team of good pals where a spirit of comradeship reigned rather like that of the old corsairs. That was the Jim Crow Squadron. No, Jean Maridor would never have any regrets that he had not been posted elsewhere. . . .

By now he must be somewhere near the English coast. He checked this with a rapid mental calculation and once more his intuition proved correct. Ahead of him the weather had cleared and in a few seconds he could make out the line of cliffs. He knew the outline of these cliffs by heart and picked out the point of the shore for which he would have to make: Folkestone. The wind had carried him slightly off his course to the south.

He recognized Folkestone and at the same time received a shock. In front of him, on the same course as himself, several aircraft rose from the sea. There were about a dozen of them. The rear ones were still nearly at sea level but he only had to follow the movement of the leaders who were rising straight in the direction of the town. And there was no mistaking the fact that these were not British aircraft. They were Focke-Wulfs. Maridor gave the information on his radio and put his supercharger in action.

In actual fact there were not a dozen but fifteen F.W.s. This scrap against fifteen German aircraft which were obviously preparing to dive-bomb Folkestone harbour, was to make Jean Maridor famous overnight throughout Great Britain. The F.W.s had also taken advantage of the bad weather to approach the Kent coast, flying at altitude zero. Each of them carried a thousand-pound bomb and had two cannon and four machine-guns in the wings. Maridor took them by surprise and immediately shot one down. The others broke formation and some of them jettisoned their bomb in the sea in order to fight with their attacker. He turned about and accepted combat, shooting down a second F.W. At that moment two Spitfires arrived to give him a helping hand and a few more F.W.s were hit. All of them except the two shot down by Maridor, however, were able to break off the action and flee. They had all dropped their bombs in the sea.

The people of Folkestone had been able to follow the combat through binoculars. On the following day a delegation visited Maridor to render him the official thanks of the town and to present him with a few bottles of magnificent French wine.

Jean Maridor never left the Jim Crow Squadron. The pilots of this group became legendary in the R.A.F. and throughout Great Britain as professionals of bad weather and lightning attacks at low altitude. When other airmen learned that one or several aircraft had penetrated with incredible audacity inside an enemy port, cannoning and machine-gunning the boats and the port defences at almost point-blank range, they said: "Those are the chaps from Jim Crow Squadron." And they were right.

And the most audacious of them all was Jean Maridor. He had even become a specialist for missions which were considered impossible. The days when the Met telephoned the station that the weather was unfit for flying, gale days when the visibility was nil, Maridor took off in his Spitfire. He penetrated all the harbours on the Belgian and French coasts from the North Sea and along the Channel to Le Havre without exception. At Le Havre he was at home and weaved among the factory chimneys and the masts of the ships. These raids made an extraordinary impression on him. At times he felt he had never left this port which he attacked from such close quarters that he could have recognized the faces of the people in the streets but for his speed.

By August, 1943, Captain Jean Maridor had shot down six enemy aircraft, personally sunk twenty ships and destroyed on the ground numerous targets of all kinds which he never even bothered to enumerate in his reports. He won the D.F.C. with bar, the Croix de Guerre with several palms, and the Croix de la Liberation.

It was at the end of this month that No. 341 Squadron, known as the "Alsace" Group, landed on Manston after a very tough engagement with the Luftwaffe over Saint-Omer and Maridor learned that the Alsace Group Commander, René Mouchotte, had not returned (René Mouchotte's body was found on the 3rd September, 1943, on the Belgian beach of Middelkerke.)

The pilots of Jim Crow Squadron continued to ply their pirate trade but the opportunity for sinking ships and shooting down aircraft just above the waves grew rarer as the German ships became less and less numerous and infrequently risked their noses out of harbour. The enemy fighters were engaged in defending Germany and the occupied territories against the great Anglo-American air offensive. Jean Maridor and his comrades deliberately crossed the channel to attack military trains, vehicles and barracks of German troops; they hardly ever met any opposition. "We must do something," said Maridor. In the spring of 1944 he was offered the command of a group which would have given him promotion. "Leave the Jim Crow Squadron?" said Maridor. "Not likely!"

The gamblers of this squadron were now excited by the

rumour that the landing was imminent and because they had just been given Spitfire 24s. This Spitfire, the last of the series, was armed with four 20mm. cannon (or two cannon and two heavy machine-guns), and had a 2,000 h.p. engine which allowed it to reach a speed of 420 m.p.h. and 100 m.p.h. faster in a slight dive. The Jim Crow pilots said that with such a "crate" they could do some good work in a battle as important as the landing, for the Luftwaffe would undoubtedly fling in all its fighters. They would certainly be given the opportunity of shooting down aircraft and increasing their own score.

They were in fact used during this battle but as we know the Luftwaffe hardly intervened. The Allies were masters of the sky and the German planes rarely put in an appearance. The Jim Crow pilots, therefore, conscientiously and with their usual skill, concentrated once more on ground targets, regretting the absence of any enemy in the air. At this time occurred the event which was completely to revolutionize their type of fighting.

On the 14th June, 1944, the first flying bomb, the V.1, fell on London. 8,070 of these bombs were to fall on England between the 13th June and the 31st August, 1944. The V.1 was a little all-metal pilotless aircraft weighing two tons, driven by jet propulsion and containing a ton of explosive. It was catapulted from a launching platform forty-five yards long. The Allied Information Service had discovered the existence of these ramps in Belgium and on the north-west coast of France and the R.A.F. had attacked and destroyed a certain number of them, but not all.

"The effect of this new German weapon made itself felt on the morale of the British," Eisenhower said, "and not on the civilians alone. The front line soldiers were anxious for their dear ones in England. The "doodle-bugs" attacked the British morale because each of them caused serious destruction wherever it fell. The population feared that there could be no defence against these new, apparently diabolical weapons."

Those responsible for the defence of London and the South of England, however, had in the meanwhile studied the question. The V.1s flew horizontally between 2,500 and 3,000 feet at a speed varying according to the wind, of between 450 and 500 m.p.h. In principle it was, therefore, impossible for the fastest fighter aircraft to attack them. The authorities worked out a defence system consisting of barrage balloons (2,000 balloons rising to a height of 6,000 feet), a zone patrolled day and night by fighter squadrons to the south and south-east of London and a coastal belt of thousands of heavy and light guns with automatic radar sighting.

"That is not enough," said one of the experts. "for the flying bombs can reach points on the coast before being destroyed by the guns or being intercepted by the fighters on the way to London. We shall have to send fighter patrols over the sea. Theirs will be the most difficult task because they will constitute the first screen against the V.1s which they will mostly have to attack before detection and at their maximum speed. But in this country we apparently have a squadron whose pilots will very quickly adapt themselves to this kind of job."

"I suppose you mean the Jim Crow Squadron," said someone.

"Precisely."

To attack a robot plane is a very spectacular action and needs particular skill. The fighter pilot at grips with an aircraft even better armed than his own is buoyed up by the idea that inside the other flying machine is a man (or perhaps several) made like himself of flesh and blood, capable, of course, of a dangerous counter-attack but also capable of weakness and error; in fact humanly vulnerable. The robot is a monster to which man has not yet become accustomed and before which he must first of all overcome a feeling of ill-ease.

The first pilots who attacked the V.1s swiftly learned that the doodle-bug, when it was hit by the shell of a fighter aircraft, exploded in the air. To hit it one had to be fairly close on account of its great speed, but one must not get too near it for in this case the explosion would also destroy the attacker.

The death or glory boys of Jim Crow Squadron found here a job which was right up their street. They cruised above the sea and as soon as they saw one of these little monsters with the rectangular wings they got into position to come parallel to its route and a little above it; then they dived and fired. This manoeuvre varied in difficulty, according to whether the V.1 had been spotted far away or at close quarters. The most delicate part of the operation consisted in opening fire at the right distance, not too close and not too far.

One of the V.1 hunters one day discovered a way of avoiding the risk of being blown to pieces by a too-near explosion of the robot. Keeping just on a level with it he approached so as to fly wing tip to wing tip. Then he engaged his wing under the wing of the V.1 and – oup ! – a flick of the wing and he turned it over. The V.1 thrown off its balance, dived into the sea.

Unfortunately the name of the man who invented this incredibly risky procedure has never been discovered. In actual fact the risk of being killed by the explosion was replaced by the risk of breaking a wing. But the V.1 hunters evolved an elegant procedure and several of them used it on every possible occasion. Jean Maridor, among others, in this way tipped several doodle-bugs into the sea. On the 2nd August, 1944, he had already destroyed or shot down ten. On the 3rd August, in the early morning, he took off to resume his chase.

It was impossible to mistake the V.1 for any other flying machine. Jean Maridor spotted one clear below him less than five miles from the shore. He manoeuvred to come in on the same course. He realized that this time he would have to attack as quickly as possible with his shells for the terrain was not suited to try the delicate operation of tipping its wing. The coast was too near and on the coast Jean Maridor could clearly distinguish the almost uninterrupted line of white spots which were inhabited houses. Thrown off its balance the robot would explode on these houses. It had to be destroyed in the air.

Jean Maridor dived and at the suitable distance fired. Since the explosive charge and the petrol tank filled the whole front part of the V.1, the explosion was usually instantaneous. But this particular one, although hit, did not explode. It began to dive earthwards towards the houses. The shells had probably only hit the mechanism of the automatic pilot. The robot, loaded with explosive, was diving at ever increasing speed. It was obvious that it would not explode until it touched the ground.

In the air the V.1 made the sound of a gigantic motor-bicycle. The coast inhabitants had become familiar with this noise; they recognized the V.1 and had seen it coming. They saw the Spitfire dive on it and even the flash of its cannon. But the V.1 had not been blown to pieces and was now diving directly upon them, accompanied by the aircraft. The two meteors approached at a terrifying speed.

Certain documents maintain that the building towards which the V.1 was diving was a hospital full of wounded men; others say it was a village. It is of no importance. Horror-struck, people watched the fatal mass hurtling down on them. They had abandoned all hope of survival when something happened that transfixed them. The aircraft in its dive drew so close to the V.1 that it almost touched. Its engine roared and once more flames spurted from its guns. There was an ear-splitting explosion and a gigantic ball of flame appeared in the sky. Then silence. A thick cloud of black smoke slowly opened, debris cascading down from its folds. One of the larger pieces spiralled lazily towards the ground. It was the wing of an aircraft.

CHAPTER THREE

"SCREWBALL" BEURLING

"Excuse me," said the young man. "can you tell me where the nearest Recruiting Office is?"

"What kind of Recruiting Office?" growled the policeman.

The young man was wearing a merchant seaman's cap and the policeman had just gone on duty at one of the dock gates in Glasgow.

"An R.A.F. Recruiting Office," explained the young man. "I want to join the R.A.F."

"That's a funny kind of accent you've got," said the policeman in broad Scots. "Are you a Canadian?"

"Yes, I am. What are the chances, do you think?"

This dialogue took place in July, 1940.

"The way things are going," the policeman said with a shrug of his shoulders, "we shall want everyone we can get in all the services. The Recruiting Office is just down this street on the right."

The young man made his way there and was received by a middle-aged officer.

"I want to join the R.A.F. as a pilot," he said. "I've done 250 flying hours."

"Canadian?" asked the officer.

"Yes, Canadian. But I think I'd better explain my case to you."

"Cerainly. Sit down."

The young man sat on the edge of his chair.

"Well, my name's Beurling — George Beurling. I'm from Lasalle, near Montreal. I wanted to join the Canadian Air Force but they wouldn't accept me because I have no university degrees. They're absolutely cracked on degrees. I've only got my pilot's certificate and 250 hours flying."

"250 hours, eh? You've already told me that once," observed the officer.

The young man shook his head. "You can't imagine

what those 250 hours mean," and, remembering that he was addressing a British officer, he added: "Sir."

"I can imagine almost anything as long as it's explained clearly to me," replied the officer.

"Okay, sir. I'll try. I've never been interested in anything else except flying. When I was nine, as soon as I came out of class I ran off to the Lasalle Road Aerodrome, which is near where I live. I couldn't take my eyes off the machines. The airfield fellows finally let me in. One day one of them said to me: 'How would you like a flip?' It seemed as though the good Lord had spoken to me. 'Well, go and ask your parents if they'll let you,' he said. I found them having dinner and said 'Can I go up in a plane?' They laughed and my mother replied 'Of course, you can fly to the moon if you want to.' They thought I was day-dreaming again."

"Naturally," nodded the officer.

"The next day I had my first taste of flying and the chap let me take the controls now and again. Later I began to build model aircraft which I sold to my pals. As soon as I had made ten dollars I ran to the airfield and hired a machine for an hour. I took over the controls at fourteen and did my first solo at sixteen."

"On what type of aircraft?" asked the officer.

"Oh, I flew Gypsy Moths and then Ramblers. I did my first loop on a Rambler far from the airfield because aerobatics were forbidden. My parents were now *au courant* and they let me fly because they realized that there was no way of stopping me. But my father refused to give me any money. I started as a workman in a wireless factory where I earned twenty-eight cents an hour. My room cost me one dollar fifty a week and my food one dollar seventy-five."

"A week?" interrupted the officer. "That's not much."

"I was interested in flying, not in eating. By making sordid economies I managed to put aside my ten dollars a week for one hour's flying. In addition to my job in the factory I became a cleaner in the aerodrome shed at night. In this way I earned a little more money and I could fly a little more. On my own, far away from the airfield, I learnt all the aerobatics one after the other – falling leaf, the Immelmann turn and the slow roll. In April, 1939, I got my pilot's certificate. My uncle then gave me five hundred dollars. I went to the aerodrome, put the money on the counter, and said to the cashier: 'Put me down for fifty hours flying.' I took and passed the commercial pilot's exam but I was told that I was too young to get a licence. So I tried to go to China."

The R.A.F. officer raised his eyebrows. "China?"

"Yes. I'd heard they needed pilots over there. I slipped across the United States frontier with the intention of embarking at San Francisco, but I didn't have the necessary papers and I wound up in prison for several weeks. When I got back to Canada, I went to see the Finnish Consul to try and join the Finnish Air Force. My parents' permission was necessary and my father would not hear of it. And then came the war. I had a crack at the Canadian Air Force. As I told you, they wouldn't have me as I have no qualifications except my pilot's certificate. I hung around for a bit and then one day a pal said to me: 'There's a ship in harbour whose captain wants sailors. Why don't you go and have a look? The ship's called the Valparaiso and it's taking munitions to Glasgow. Once you get there you're certain to be able to join the R.A.F.' I hurried aboard the Valparaiso. The captain said that he was sailing in half an hour but that he needed a deck hand. I said okay and that's how I got here. Off the coast of Ireland we met a U-boat pack and seven cargo ships were torpedoed in ten minutes, but luckily for me not the Valparaiso. I hope you're not going to ask me for my school certificate, sir."

"Not necessarily," replied the officer, "but I imagine you've got some papers on you – a birth certificate, for example. Besides, you've entered England illegally, if you have no papers. You could be arrested at any moment."

"Hell, you're not going to have me arrested!" cried George Beurling. "I came here to join the R.A.F."

"I shan't have you arrested," replied the officer. "I have other things to do. But, once more, I can't do anything for you if you haven't got any papers."

George Beurling picked up his cap which he had left on the ground beside his chair.

"Good," he said. "I'll go and fetch them."

He spoke as if he only had to cross the street. In actual fact he sailed back across the Atlantic in the *Valparaiso*. He disembarked at Montreal and on this trip only one cargo boat in the convoy was sunk.

"Don't upset yourself," he said to his stupefied parents. "I'm only just passing through. I've come to fetch my papers to join the R.A.F. in Glasgow."

"The R.A.F.?" cried his mother. "But you're crazy. You can just as well join the infantry here or the tanks."

George Beurling shrugged his shoulders. "I thought you'd have understood by now that I want to fly. Besides there's only one service where I have a chance of getting through and that's the air force. I should get killed in the tanks or in the infantry."

He remained at home for five days and this time his father helped him to get the necessary papers. On the 8th August, 1940, the *Valparaiso* put to sea again loaded with munitions and with George Beurling aboard. None of the ships in the convoy were sunk. She docked at Glasgow during an air raid warning. Beurling jumped ashore; a policeman stopped him. "Where are you off to like that? Good God, it's you again."

It was the same policeman.

"Yes, it's me again," replied Beurling. "I'm going to the Recruiting Office. I know the way."

The officer raised his head when he saw him come in. It was the same officer. "Well, I'm damned," he cried. "It's my Canadian!"

"Yes," said Beurling, "here are my papers and here's the birth certificate."

George Beurling signed on. The following period was not very pleasant. Instead of flying he began to drill in a depot under the orders of sergeants who would not listen to his 250 hours flying time. He also had to fill in the bomb holes left by the German bombers on an airfield near London. About this time he learned by chance that the *Valparaiso* had been sunk in the Atlantic on her return trip. "Well," thought Beurling, "I might be worse off."

He was then sent to an initial training wing where he had to spend a great part of his time in mathematics, navigation and at the Met. His pilot's experience only began to count when he was sent to the elementary flying training school. There the instructors had to admit that this boy was really talented in regard to flying. But this gift was not enough to make a fighter pilot. He still had to pass through other schools and other training centres to learn night flying, formation flying, blind flying and how to shoot. During the course of these long classes, Beurling had some trouble with the discipline but not a single accident. On 16th December, 1941, he was promoted sergeant pilot and posted to No. 403 squadron, 2nd fighter group.

By May, 1942, George Beurling had two victories to his credit. He had taken part in bomber escorts and raids over France. Flying his Spitfire with consummate skill, he had shot down his two opponents with a single burst. On several occasions his undoubted flying talents allowed him to get out of some extremely tough spots. His squadron leader asked him if he had any ambition to become an officer.

"No, thanks, sir," replied Beurling. "I've some very good pals among the sergeants."

During this May month, 1942, however, George Beurling was not happy. To begin with, No. 403 squadron was transformed into an all-Canadian unit and he, as a Canadian, had to leave it because he had joined the R.A.F. instead of the Royal Canadian Air Force. In his new unit there were only Britishers with whom he did not get on too well. His messmates reproached him for a frankness which they considered excessive.

A more serious reproach was that he had outraged formation flight discipline by shooting down his second plane. As I have already mentioned, this discipline was a golden rule in the R.A.F. and close formation was considered the best method of defence. Beurling had shown too much individualism. In the eyes of the other pilots his second victory had been won at the expense of flight solidarity.

In the mess hardly anyone spoke to him.

On the 21st May, 1942, one of the pilots was chosen to be transferred overseas. The choice fell upon a young married man whose wife was expecting a baby. He did not hide the fact that he was not overjoyed at the prospect of being sent far away – the order did not specify where.

"If I can manage to replace you, would you agree?" asked Beurling.

The newly-married man was delighted.

"The candidate has to be able to take off from an aircraft carrier," the squadron commander said to Beurling. "Could you do it?"

"Yes, sir."

On the following day George Beurling arrived at the embarkation depot where he found thirty-six other pilots with whom he was to sail in a cargo ship. In the holds were thirty-six Spitfires. The ship, escorted by a destroyer and a corvette, put to sea at once for an unknown destination. A few days later it entered Gibraltar Harbour and there the pilots found that their destination was Malta.

The streets of Gibraltar were brightly lit at night as in peacetime. In all the restaurants one could order huge steaks, cakes and fresh fruit. The change from the Spartan diet of Great Britain was very welcome.

For two days the pilots thoroughly enjoyed themselves. On the morning of June 7th, thirty-three of them, including Beurling, received orders to report at 18.00 hours on board the aircraft carrier *Eagle*. The Spitfires were already aboard. The *Eagle* sailed at eight o'clock in the morning.

During the afternoon a Wing Commander briefed the pilots.

"You will take off tomorrow morning at 06.00 hours in groups of eight," he told them. "You will fly south-east until you see the Tunisian coast, then south to this point on the map and from there you will set an easterly course. You have 745 miles to cover in all. Absolute radio silence except in case of distress, when you can transmit. 'May Day'. At first you will receive messages from the aircraft carrier and later from Malta. On take-off open the throttle full and keep your brakes on until your tail is up. At that moment, off you go. Goodnight."

The take-off took place as arranged, Beurling with the third group. At 09.30 hours at 21,000 feet he saw a clear flat rock in the middle of the sea – Malta. Fifty minutes later he landed with his group on Takali airfield while it was being bombed.

The ack-ack was firing furiously; several dog fights were taking place over the island and out to sea. Parachutes continued to open amid the ack-ack bursts. Aircraft fell in flames, others dived with a thunderous roar. Rescue launches sped over the water to pick up the pilots who had been shot down.

The Spitfires which had just arrived taxied towards the hangars along runways pitted with bomb craters and strewn with the debris of aircraft. Their pilots spent their first quarter of an hour in Malta in the shelters and aerodrome trenches; they were covered with dust and clods of earth thrown up by the explosion.

"It's like this nearly every day," said Wing Commander Gracey. "Don't imagine you're in for a picnic. You've just seen your comrades cover your arrival. Tomorrow it'll be your turn. Keep your eyes well skinned if you want to remain alive for a bit, and now I'll show you to your quarters." The N.C.O. pilots' quarters were in an old tunnel-shaped chalk-quarry, five miles from the airfield. Here Beurling found Englishmen, Americans, Australians, New Zealanders and one Canadian.

"The most unpleasant thing here," a New Zealander said to him, "is the food. Corned beef, corned beef, the whole bloody time!"

"What's the gen here?" asked Beurling.

The New Zealander explained.

Malta possessed both an offensive and a defensive air force. The former consisted of twenty torpedo-carrying aircraft and thirty bombers which attacked the axis convoys as often as they could. During 1941 this handful of constantly replaced aircraft had destroyed more than half the German and Italian tonnage in the Mediterranean.

This is why the German and Italian Air Forces (600 bombers and fighters concentrated in Sicily) pounded Malta as though they would have liked to wipe it off the face of the ocean.

The British fleet had long since deserted the smashed port of Valetta where rare convoys arrived at long intervals after losing fifty or sixty of their effectives. The severely rationed population lived in the rocky caves of the island. The German radio referred to them as the two hundred and fifty thousand prisoners of Malta. Between raids the Maltese went about their ordinary business. The operations room, which received radar information about the approaching enemy formations and gave orders to the fighters to take off, was also installed in a huge cave. The day Beurling's Spitfires arrived, Malta had only fifteen fighters left for its aerial defence.

"We are very pleased to see you here," said the New Zealander, "but you must realize that things don't go on here as in England. We get up at four in the morning and take the bus at half-past four to the airfield, where we stay at action stations in the dispersal pen at the edge of the runway. As soon as the Tannoy gives 'Scramble!' we jump out of the windows, run to our crates and get in the air. Then we have to bring down as many Germans and Italians as possible without being brought down ourselves. As we are always outnumbered we have to get by as best we can."

"That's the kind of work I like," said Beurling.

From the 12th June onwards the new Malta pilots could see for themselves some of the strange conditions of air combat above the island. At seven o'clock they were in their dispersal pens drinking hot chocolate when the loud-speakers announced: "Scramble for four aircraft!"

The four pilots on duty in order of rotation were soon airborne. Ops transmitted on the radio: "Gain height as quickly as possible!"

Ten minutes later they had reached 18,000 feet. At this moment ops reported: "Fifteen enemy aircraft approaching from Zukor point at twenty-one to twenty-two thousand feet. No big job."

The phrase "No big job" merely meant that the enemy

formation contained no bombers. It was not out of contempt for the enemy that the air force commander at Malta sent only four Spitfires against fifteen enemy fighters: it was to economize fuel.

The four Spitfires (Beurling flying one of them) advanced in single line, a convenient formation for each pilot could observe his comrades tail. But this formation was not kept for very long. A dog fight with the Me 109s soon developed. Beurling set the tail of a Messerschmitt on fire and it crashed into the sea. Since no one except himself saw it sink (the other pilots were fully occupied) this adversary was only counted as damaged.

Less than ten minutes after the start of the engagement the visitors – minus Beurling's victim – set their course for Sicily. The Spitfires did not pursue them, not from lack of courage but in accordance with orders to economize fuel.

After this first battle an event occurred which had not been seen at Malta for some months, in fact for ages: ten days passed without a single enemy attack.

At first the newcomers wondered if the old hands had not made their descriptions too lurid. But a few days later they revised their opinion. It was obvious, and it showed even more during this period of calm, that the nervous state of some of the old ones left much to be desired. Some showed themselves excessively talkative and others abnormally silent, while a few were very irritable. Those who had stuck it out best explained to the newcomers that from time to time a pilot would begin in an obsessive manner to discuss the statistics and percentage of losses in the fighter unit. Wing Commander Gracey was then notified and he sent the pilot on leave. It was an understood thing in any case that a pilot could not remain more than three or four months at Malta – if he survived that long.

During this period of calm Beurling and his comrades bathed in the blue Mediterranean round the rocks of Malta or the little nearby island of Gozo, which was half its size and almost deserted.

The enemy aircraft began to show themselves once more on the 25th June. By the 6th July everyone felt that the axis had decided to continue the bombardment of Malta very seriously.

At eight o'clock three bombers escorted by three Macchis were reported. Beurling was a member of the patrol sent to deal with this formation. With his first burst he hit one of the bombers, then seeing one of the Macchis on the tail of a comrade he gave him two bursts which dispatched him in flames towards the sea. A few seconds later he fired another burst and a second Macchi exploded.

The same evening Beurling took off again with a patrol ordered to beat off two Junkers 88 escorted by twenty Messerschmitts. In the course of the fight he shot down one of the Messerschmitts with a single burst. His score for that day was two Macchis and one Messerschmitt shot down and a bomber damaged.

To the writer, Leslie Roberts, who questioned him later at great length about the sensation of aerial combat "Screwball" Beurling replied: "I didn't feel anything in particular. No, I wasn't tired. Proud of my success? No, I just thought I was lucky."

"And did they congratulate you on your return to the Mess? Did they lay on a party for you?"

"No, that evening Gracey merely said: 'Good show, Beurling!'" Actually you thought more of thanking the pal who had chased an enemy off your tail than of congratulating him on his personal score.

In actual fact, one can deduce from other testimonies that Beurling, like most fighter pilots, was always very proud of his victories. But he had obviously been affected by the disapproval of his British comrades after his second victory and wanted to show that he understood the team spirit.

The offensive against Malta continued furiously during the month of July, broken by a relative calm for a few days after the 15th. The enemy formations sometimes consisted of as many as 87 bombers escorted by 50 fighters. The Spitfires were continually at action stations and took off several times a day.

Those bombers which had managed to escape interception – it was not possible to stop them all – dropped their loads on the airfields, the harbour and the town. Three-quarters of the latter were in ruins. Fortunately the Malta caves were bomb-proof and fires found little to feed on in this treeless rock with its stone houses. The population suffered more from hunger than the bombing.

"Screwball" Beurling fought every day with his comrades. When one reads the reports of his air battles one is amazed by the speed with which he disposed of the enemy. In nearly every case a single burst of one or two seconds was enough. He has given his own reasons for this efficiency.

"You can be the best and most accurate pilot in the world, but if you're a bad shot you'll never shoot down the enemy. On the other hand, if you are the best shot in the world and you're not a good pilot the enemy will shoot you down." It would seem that Beurling, if not the best pilot and the best shot in the world, was at least one of the best.

Between the 6th and 29th July, 1942, he shot down fifteen enemy aircraft (four on the 29th alone) and damaged five. On the 29th he was promoted Pilot Officer. He was awarded the D.F.M. on the 15th.

At the end of July only seven of the twenty-three pilots who had arrived with Beurling in Malta were left. Eight had been killed in battle, the others evacuated on account of wounds or for rest.

Among the dead was a pilot with whom Beurling had been great friends, a Canadian named Jean Paradis. Beurling and he bathed together on quiet days and lay in the sun on the white rocks beside the dazzling Mediterranean, talking of their far-off homeland. Fighter pilot Beurling, to whom nothing seemed to count except flying and fighting, retained a precious memory of those hours, strange interludes of peace in the midst of the fury of war.

Now Jean Paradis was dead. Other pilots had arrived to replace the missing and the evacuated, and of these new arrivals some of them already no longer existed. Wing Commander Gracey had been sent back to Great Britain to rest and had been replaced by Wing Commander Grant. On the 9th August, Lord Gort, Governor of Malta, was informed that a convoy was leaving Gibraltar to supply the island.

This convoy was composed of fourteen cargo ships and tankers escorted by several warships, one of which was an aircraft carrier. It was attacked uninterruptedly by aircraft and by packs of submarines after the longitude of Cape Bon. The aircraft from the carrier defended it as best they could and then the Malta Spitfires joined in as the battle grew nearer.

On the 11th August, the Maltese saw six cargo ships, nearly all damaged by torpedoes or by bombs, limp one after the other into the damaged port of Valetta. This was all that remained of the convoy. The warships received orders to turn round immediately. The military authorities of Malta were distressed to see that not a single tanker had reached harbour.

Two days later, however, one arrived. The only survivor. Torpedoed on the previous evening, it had crawled along at three knots, having lost the convoy and the escort. When it was sighted the Spitfires took off to protect it. With a terrible list to starboard it looked like a hulk. The thousands of gallons of fuel it carried in its flank were more precious than food to Malta.

George Beurling did not take part in this convoy battle, and he was only able to fly and fight intermittently during August. He spent several days in hospital with an attack of dysentery known as "Malta dog", which is caused by the vegetables on the island: these grow on a very small strip of land which is over-manured with nitrates.

George Beurling suffered more with "Malta dog" on the ground than in the air, for the intake of oxygen helped him. On certain days the doctors pronounced him unfit and he had to submit. For this reason he was only able to shoot down a single enemy plane from the beginning of August to the 25th September, the day when he shot down two.

During this period the Spitfires had carried out several offensive operations against the Sicilian airfields, machine-gunning and destroying enemy aircraft on the ground or at the moment of take-off. But from the beginning of

October the inhabitants of Malta realized that this month was going to be as tough for them as had been the month of July.

No convoy had succeeded in reaching the island since the one on the 11th August. Lord Gort had set up communal kitchens. All the goats had been slaughtered, although they were the only source of fresh milk on the island. This was done both for the meat and to avoid having to feed them. The 1,500 odd civilians who had remained in Valetta itself spent most of their lives in the caves. Water was rationed and only the hospital was allowed to use the electric current. Infant mortality rose in August to 418 per 1,000 and to 425 per 1,000 in September.

The enemy raids continued at the same rhythm of three or four a day. George Beurling fought whenever the "Malta dog" did not render him unfit. On the evening of the 13th October his score over Malta reached 24 (26 in all).

All the fighters of Takali and Luqa airfields took off together on the midday of the 14th October to intercept eight Junkers 88s escorted by fifty fighters. Beurling was one of the party.

At 21,000 feet he spotted the enemy planes coming from the east. Over the intercom he cried to his co-pilot, Heather, "Wade in!" Each of them dived on a Junkers. A few seconds later the two Germans were in flames and spinning seawards.

At this moment Beurling noticed that eight Messerschmitts were on Heather's tail just below him. "Look behind you, Red!" he cried, and dived. As he passed near the bomber to which he had just set fire the rear-gunner fired on him. Beurling felt he had been hit in the hand and the left forearm, but not seriously. He fired a long, carefully aimed burst from 400 yards at one of the Messerschmitts which was chasing his friend. The German began to smoke and went into a spin. The others broke off the action. Heather was now out of danger. Beurling's aircraft was hit by two bursts, one in each wing. He pulled his stick and opened his throttle, trying to gain height for a moment above the milling fight and to see clearly. Suddenly he heard an anxious voice in the intercom.

"Send someone to Kalafrana Bay to give us a hand. There are two of us against twenty Messerschmitts!"

Beurling was just above the bay. He dived his damaged aircraft, pulled out just below a Messerschmitt which was preparing to fire on a Spitfire. He recognized the Spitfire. It was Willy the Kid, one of his real pals. Beurling felt his heart beat faster. With a two-second burst he cut off the Messerschmitt's left wing at the fuselage and the German spun down.

"There's a golden rule in this game if you want to stay alive," Beurling declared to Leslie Roberts. "Always look behind you before attacking. This time, and it was the first time, I didn't do it."

He felt a shock in his right heel and at practically the same moment realized that a burst had entered between his left arm and his body, wounding him seriously on the elbow and the right side. His controls would no longer respond. He had been attacked from behind and below.

The throttle was at maximum gate and his aircraft dived at full power from 18,000 feet. Beurling opened the cockpit with the intention of baling out. The wind produced by this plummeting descent glued him to his seat.

"I was resigned at first. Well, I thought, this is the chopper. But I soon found myself struggling."

He managed to get out of the cockpit and to climb on to the left wing. The slipstream transfixed him there. The blue sea below sped rapidly upwards. At 1,500 feet he managed to slip off. He felt himself fall and thought *Can I pull the ripcord now?* He pulled it; the parachute opened with a terrible report but did not tear.

Beurling descended gently towards the sea. The sudden impression of calm was extraordinary. A Spitfire circled him and then flew off. The moment he touched the water he jettisoned his parachute and found himself floating, supported by his Mae West jacket, while his dinghy began to blow up. He hitched himself into it. After a few minutes he noticed that the bottom of the rubber dinghy was full of blood. But an airsea rescue craft arrived, throwing up a huge wake of white foam.

His friends were quick to visit him in hospital.

"I shan't be in here for very long," he said. "My wounds are not serious."

"Of course not. You've always been a luck guy."

But the "Malta dog" and the lack of vitamins had seriously weakened this "lucky guy's" constitution. His heel was infected and several months were to elapse before this wound consented to close.

The blitz over Malta continued. Beurling could hear the bombing from his bed. Sometimes he dragged himself to the window to watch the dog fights. Other wounded comrades arrived. The hospital was full of pilots. On the 25th October, Air Vice Marshal Park, R.A.F. Commander in Malta, came up to Beurling's bed.

"We've just had a message from London," he said. "You've been awarded the D.S.O. There was also a message from the Canadian Government asking that you should be sent back home to convalesce. You will help the recruiting and the propaganda."

"Thank you very much, sir, but I think in about a fortnight I shall be able to fly again."

"I think it will be a little longer than that, Beurling."

The citation accompanying the D.S.O. recalled that Beurling's score had risen to 28 victories plus three probables and concluded: "The skill and courage of this pilot are unsurpassed."

But "Screwball" Beurling's adventures were not yet over.

Two days later his Wing Commander came to visit him in hospital.

"You're leaving this evening for Gibraltar," he said, "in a Liberator. You'll have plenty of friends with you, among them Heather and Willy the Kid. They haven't forgotten that you probably saved their lives. What about coming over to the Mess at Takali to pick up your things and say good-bye?"

After the farewell dinner Beurling and his pals went to Luqa airfield. The contingent to be evacuated comprised twenty-six pilots, three civilians plus seven women and two babies: forty-two people including the Liberator's crew of six. The sky was overcast.

"Sorry," said the pilot of the transport plane, "but the Met gives very bad weather to the west and I can't take you direct to Gibraltar. But in the east it's okay so I shall just slip across to Aexandria and take on some freights for Malta. I'll pick you up later."

The civilians returned home and the pilots settled down as best they could in the Luqa Mess. Four days elapsed. The air raid warnings and the bombing continued and the news of the battles came through. Pilot So-and-so had to crash-land. So-and-so had been killed.

The Liberator finally appeared during the night of the 31st. It took the air with its load of evacuees on the 1st November at three in the morning. At dawn the sky was clear and the sea blue. Not a ship in sight, not an aircraft. The war seemed to have vanished.

They ran into clouds before Gibraltar and the famous rock appeared through the rain. The Liberator circled to make his run in, but disturbed by the air currents round the rock he landed in the middle of the runway and bounced. The pilot had to go round again. "It was very disagreeable," said Beurling. "I began to undo my heavy flying suit very quickly."

The Liberator returned over the sea and gained height. Suddenly at about 50 feet it stalled and fell.

Beurling had opened a door just to the right of the seat and at the moment the aircraft touched the water he leapt, followed by two or three others. The aircraft broke up and sank almost immediately. Nothing could be seen on the surface except some debris to which men were clinging. Beurling tried to recognize them in the weak dawn light. He heard someone cry: "If you can make the coast, get going."

Supported by his Mae West and encumbered by his bandaged foot, Beurling managed to make his way towards land, which seemed fairly near. Rescue was already at hand. Some soldiers ran down to the shore carrying stretchers. Beurling touched firm ground and felt himself supported by the shoulders.

"There are wounded men out there who can't swim,"

he told the soldiers, "and women and children."

The door of the ambulance had already closed on him. Not until that evening, lying once more in a hospital bed, did Beurling know the balance sheet of the accident: fifteen dead or missing, among them three civilians, two women and two babies. Heather and Willy the Kid were among the missing.

From his bed Beurling could see the lights of Gibraltar gleaming in the night. Despite the war and the dead, life went on. He thought of Jean Paradis with whom he had bathed in the blue transparent water, of all his comrades who had been killed, and of those who had just been drowned like cats in the hull of the Liberator, those who had conquered death so many times in the sky. "I watched the Gibraltar lights all night, trying to find some meaning in it all."

He did not yet know that the war was over for him and no one could have foreseen that his destiny would be to kill himself, as did so many of his friends, in an aircraft two years after the end of the war.

Demobilized, this adventurer who only knew how to fly had found a job which was bound to please him: transporting arms to the State of Israel. The job was not without risks or without profits, and many picturesque types could be found among the pilots. The aircraft were old types bought from American surplus stocks. On an Autumn day in 1947 one of them stalled on taking off from Rome, crashed and exploded. It was loaded to the limit with arms and ammunition, like the old tramp ship *Valparaiso* in which Beurling had come to Europe for the first time. Beurling was piloting it.

CHAPTER FOUR

FRUITLESS VICTORIES

AT midday on the 23rd November, 1939, a single-seater Curtiss fighter with French tricolour cockades took off from Suippes airfield and after gaining height made off in a north-easterly direction. At 6,000 feet the aircraft was completely clear of the light autumnal mist. The sky above was a dazzling blue.

At 12,000 feet the pilot adjusted his oxygen tube. He looked down at his thigh, to which was fastened a large-scale map stuck on to a piece of inner tubing.

Varennes-en-Argonne, he thought. *Everything O.K.*

He uttered a few words into the inside of his mask and the laryngophone fixed on to his neck transmitted the vibrations. On the ground, forty miles away, the C.O. of a fighter group tuned in in his radio car heard the insect giving its position in the conventional language.

The aircraft continued to climb in the direction of the Meuse. His flying orders read: "Patrol *a priori* on a line Verdun-Montmédy." A *priori* meant that no enemy had been sighted. It was a routine patrol to observe the sector.

A routine patrol normally comprised three aircraft; a light patrol two. The Squadron Commander had decided to dispatch single aircraft patrols in order to spare the personnel. Apart from flying hours the pilots, according to the regulations, could be either at action stations, in readiness, or at rest. Action stations meant that the pilots sat in their aircraft in full flying gear with the engines warm. Every half an hour the engines were revved up. The aircraft in readiness had to be airborne half an hour after receiving their orders. The personnel was on the spot or in the immediate vicinity. When resting the pilots had to be able to take off within two hours.

Now, since each squadron (two flights) had to maintain a permanent flight (in practice nine available aircraft) at action stations and another in readiness, the rest period laid down by madly optimistic regulations had never existed since mobilization. The pilots were constantly on a roster either at action stations in readiness, or on high altitude patrol.

Only on high altitude patrol was there a possibility of intercepting the Dornier 17s and Dornier 215s which crossed the frontier. These big German aircraft were magnificent twin-engined bombers but they never dropped bombs, only pamphlets. Sometimes they took photographs.

A magnificent sight now met the eyes of the Curtiss pilot: the winding ribbon of the Meuse against the dark green of the forests, ploughed fields and the towns which the "phoney" war had left intact – Sédan, Rocroi, Givet. . . . At 21,000 feet the ribbon of the Moselle appeared to the east; beyond it the dark green crests of the Vosges, separated by valleys of milky mist. The pilot turned his head completely to starboard to look at other heights, remote but magnificently outlined, their snowy peaks emerging from the mist of the horizon, hundreds of miles away – the Alps. Then once more he consulted his map and the instruments on his panel. The altimeter needle continued to move slowly. The hands of his watch also moved forward. . . .

Before the war the experts maintained that no aviator should fly above 25,000 feet more than once a month. The strain on the human organs, they said, was too dangerous. Now, for an hour, the pilot's altimeter had registered 27,000 feet and all the pilots of his squadron carried out a similar mission every day and sometimes twice a day. In each consecutive war they discover that the human body can stand far more than they imagined.

The thermometer registered the temperature outside the cabin as −50°C. Inside the cockpit it must have been −15°C. The pilot was protected by his insulated flying suit; the electric points of this suit functioned badly for the French system had been hastily adapted to the American Curtiss aircraft. It was very cold.

The pilot's eyes now began to suffer and he saw tiny butterflies coming towards him from all sides. With his icy-cold hand he opened the tap of the rear cylinder, the others now being empty. This trifling effort nearly exhausted him. He turned his inhaler to the position "strong flow". More oxygen came through and revived him.

The nearer the end of his mission approached the slower the hand of his watch seemed to advance. But at last the moment came.

I shall climb a little to see at what height vapour trails are produced, he decided, and then I'll return to base.

He opened his throttle wide. At 30,000 feet the engine began to cough but the aircraft climbed slowly to 31,000. The pilot glanced behind him. His aircraft was trailing a long dazzling silver white mane in the icy air. Below a certain temperature the particles of water subject to condensation on leaving the exhaust pipes crystallized and formed this vapour trail.

The pilot in question was Capitaine Jean Accart, commanding 1/5 Squadron stationed at that time at Suippes. The tactical unit of fighter aircraft was the wing. But each squadron possessed an outstanding personality. 1/5 was the new designation of the old SPA 67 from the 1914–18 War. The squadron tradition had been maintained, almost religiously, a thing which often happens in military units in all countries. On their fuselages the aircraft of 1/5 sported a stork with lowered wings on a black and orange flag. This emblem had been given to SPA 67 in 1916 by Capitaine de Villepin who had come from SPA 3, Guynemer's squadron. Thus the 1/5 ex-SPA 67 was, according to the conventional traditions, the godchild of SPA 3 and was part of the illustrious "Stork Wing".

During the winter of 1939–1940, Capitaine Accart, in common with all the pilots of the north-east air front, took part in these monotonous and exhausting high altitude patrols. During the one just described, at the very moment he set course for home he caught sight of, pursued and engaged a Dornier 17 which eventually managed to escape.

In November, 1939, none of the belligerents had yet dropped a single bomb on their adversaries. As yet no aircraft had dived with a roar on the opposing troops which for the moment were content with patrol skirmishes. There was no bombing. This was the tacit understanding. But the aircraft which met each other in the sky fought in deadly earnest. The French fighters engaged the German reconnaissance planes and the Messerschmitt 109s which sometimes escorted them. Other encounters took place between French and German fighters on patrol over the lines. During those first three months of war about sixty German aircraft were shot down and a dozen French pilots were killed. One of these was Capitaine Claude, commanding No. 1 squadron of fighter wing II/4.

Pierre Claude was born on the 10th October, 1910, at Antananarivo where his father administered the colony of Madagascar. When his mother returned with him to France fifteen months later the child had never uttered a word. They thought that he was dumb in spite of his wide-awake expression. In the station at Marseilles, seeing the express arrive, the baby clapped its hands and cried out distinctly: "The train." His mother wept.

Between the ages of four and six, Pierre Claude suffered from severe attacks of asthma which periodically kept him away from his studies and games. At the age of ten he had an emergency operation for a punctured appendix and at fourteen he nearly died of double pneumonia. Nevertheless he was a brilliant success at school. When he was asked what profession he would choose, he replied. "I shall go to Saint-Cyr and from there into the Armée de l'Air."

He received his air baptism at the age of nine and built a host of model aeroplanes. His parents were in doubt as to whether his frail health would one day allow him to realize his dream, but he himself had no doubts on this score. He had enormous confidence in his energy and even more in God. His faith was very much alive and his vocation as an aviator appeared to him almost a religious one. At twenty-one he entred Saint-Cyr. He was convinced that he had won a decisive victory over his weak frame the day he obtained his pilot's certificate.

"Why do you want to be a fighter pilot at all costs?" his mother wrote to him. "I should be less worried if you chose bombers. After all you are less exposed there."

"In a bomber," Claude replied, "I might, without knowing it, murder women and children. As a fighter I shall always be fighting a man."

On the 25th September, 1939, Captaine Claude, with two other pilots attacked a formation of Messerschmitts. While his comrades fought and shot down two enemy aircraft he found himself separated from them and involved in a dog fight with two or three of the enemy who were soon joined by several others. He did not break off the engagement, shooting down one of the Messerschmitts and chasing the others across the enemy lines. At this moment his engine caught fire.

He had time to return to the French lines but he was now pursued by the Messerschmitts which attacked his damaged Curtiss. From the ground he was seen to bale out and they saw his parachute open. But when he landed he was dead with two bullets through his forehead. One of the enemy had fired on him while he was coming down by parachute. During the whole course of the war in the air there were very few cases of such a cowardly act; it was considered degrading by the War pilots of all countries.

The aerial combats of the "phoney" war, even when two fighters were in single combat, were unequal in regard to armament. The Messerschmitt 109, in service at the start of hostilities, was superior (except in manoeuvrability) to all the French or naturalized French aircraft, including the Curtiss to which it was greatly superior in climb. And on the 21st November, the French pilots saw appear in the sky for the first time the new version of the Me 109s whose horizontal speed of 345 m.p.h. was 40 m.p.h. faster than the Curtiss and whose climbing speed was astonishing. "The differences in speed are so great that the Messerschmitt can refuse battle without manoeuvring by merely opening the throttle," wrote Commandant Hugues, O.C. Fighter Wing II/5 on the 23rd November.

As for the Morane 406 in service with twelve squadrons, its superiority in speed over the German bomber aircraft used as "recce" planes was so insignificant (about 6 m.p.h.) that the pilots often had to abandon an engagement with these photographing aircraft when they saw them flying off in the distance. There was no chance of catching them.

They could only report their position to their ground comrades over the radio. This enabled them to send faster aircraft or aircraft better placed for interception. The Wing Commander turned the dials on his panel tuned in to the radio.

"*Hallo. Hallo.* 43-B-2, here 0/03 calling. Can you hear me?"

"Here 43-B-21. I can hear you. Over to you."

The C.O. began in the regulation language to give his message reporting the German aircraft.

"*Hallo.* 43-B-21. Repeat."

Sometimes the communication proceeded normally but at others the radio began to splutter and they could hear nothing. By this time the enemy "recce" plane was already far away.

In the upper regions of the icy sky, the fighters pursued their monotonous, thankless, exhausting vigil. To resist the temptation of losing a little height in order to breathe better and to suffer less from the cold, sometimes required more will power than that demanded by aerial combat.

On the ground, life was rarely amusing during the winter of the "phoney" war. The legendary squadron bar was often housed in a gloomy hutment. Each day at dawn the engines had to be warmed up with the help of the "bellows car" which sent warm air (more or less warm because the apparatus was by no means perfect) beneath the cowling. One or several pilots took off, others got into their flying suits, others go on sleeping, waiting for their turn at action stations or their operational orders.

The fighter pilot must never lack food or sleep unless he wishes to go into battle in a state of inferiority. When the depth of winter had passed and the days lengthened, sleep was doled out more and more parsimoniously to the inadequate number of pilots in most of the French fighter groups. There were several accidents due entirely to physical weakness. But there was no remedy for this state of affairs and the necessities of the "hot war" would soon force them to sweep away all precautions which had so far been considered indispensable concerning the human frame. Fortunately most of the pilots were unaware of the numerical condition of inequality in which they were to wage this "hot war" in the air: 400 outclassed French aircraft had to stand up to an air fleet of 3,500 bombers, protected by 1,500 fighters.

On the 10th May, 1940, from 3.45 a.m. onwards, an immense roar spread through the dark sky above the north-north-eastern Front. This was the German bomber stream escorted by Messerschmitts.

On the French fighter airfields where no orders, no alarm had yet been given, the pilots of the dawn patrol, already in their equipment, were ready to climb into their aircraft while the mechanics started up the engines to warm them. From time to time the engines fell silent. The pilots were waiting for daybreak. Everyone listened. The great roar continued overhead.

Three light patrols from Squadron 1/5 took off at daybreak with Capitaine Jean Accart in command of the third. He had asked and obtained permission to fly over his usual sector which covered the Second Army. The aircraft were swallowed up in the thin layer of ground mist as soon as they were airborne. Capitaine Accart's patrol met the enemy – fifteen Me 110s flying in flights of three – above the valley of the Meuse. The Me 110 was a twin-engined fighter, armed with two 20 mm. cannon, four front and one rear machine-guns; it had a maximum speed of 356 m.p.h. Capitaine Accart decided to engage. The great principle of aerial combat is to attack the enemy from the rear. But the victim knows this perfectly well and manoeuvres in turn to get on his opponent's tail. This is precisely what the Me 110s did that morning. Hardly had the attack begun than they manoeuvred to get on the tail of the two Curtisses. Capitaine Accart then decided to meet them head on. He did a swift, climbing turn to get into position.

The first Messerschmitt loomed large in his gonio. Capitaine Accart saw spurts of flame leaving its machine-guns and cannon as he fired. *Houp!* The German leaped into the air. Now for the next. ... The bullets of the two adversaries split the air at the same time. *Houp!* The second Messerschmitt leapt in turn. No question of looking back to see if he had been hit or not, for already the third aircraft was in his sights. The life of the fighter pilot is at stake in this fraction of a second during which the tracers cross. The pilot had not even time to think.

Each time one of the Germans jumped over him, Capitaine Accart caught the following one in his gonio, saw it increase in size and pressed his firing button. After the fifth, all that remained was the empty sky. The extraordinary game of leap-frog was over. Accart banked to return to the formation but the Messerschmitts were already far away, growing smaller at every second.

The radio began to crackle. Capitaine Accart recognized the voice of Adjutant-Chef Bouvard, who gave his code name. Bouvard was calling "Nadia" the radio car.

"We are in contact with five Dorniers over Mourmelon. 12,000 feet, flying north-east."

The two Curtisses of Accart's patrol went into a shallow dive, reaching 400 m.p.h. A moment later Bouvard announced that a damaged bomber was being chased by Sous-Lieutenant Goupy. Capitaine Accart could already see the other Do 17s. One of them was straggling slightly to port. Every aircraft which leaves its formation, even slightly, must know what will happen. It is automatically chosen as target. The fate of this one was decided in three minutes. The two Curtisses, in line alternately, pumped their deadly bursts into it. Like its comrade it crash-landed to the north of Valmy. The German crew set fire to their aircraft.

On his return to Suippes, Capitaine Accart learned the exact significance of the gigantic roar which had filled the heavens before dawn. At daybreak, formations of German twin-engined aircraft had bombarded numerous airfields and railway installations on the line to the east. On the whole, these attacks had caused less damage than might have been expected, since the early morning fog had interfered with their aim. The alarm system had functioned very badly. In nearly every case the arrival of the enemy had been announced by the falling of the bombs. Suippes airfield had not been strafed.

Several fighter squadrons were airborne before the first attack, to carry out patrols ordered the previous night or on the initiative of their commanding officers who had been warned by the passage of the enemy bombers. Others had to take off from airfields pitted with bomb craters and among blazing hangars.

The German armies had invaded Holland, Belgium and Luxemburg. The real war had started. The cavalry of the Second Army had retreated before the German armour but advanced elements of the Seventh Army crossed the Belgian Frontier to make a stand against the enemy. The original plan had been put into operation and the General Staff seemed optimistic. The airmen said nothing. They merely stated that in the air the enemy aircraft were surprisingly numerous, rapid and well armed.

By the end of the morning Squadron 1/5 received orders to send a patrol to protect a Potez 63 on reconnaissance reporting the position of cavalry units of the Second Army. The mission was carried out without incident except above Arlon on the Belgo-Luxemburg Frontier. The aircraft saw the fireworks of tracer bullets rising from the ground. Flak batteries had already been installed there. On the roads an uninterrupted procession of armoured columns, German columns en route for the West. ... This spectacle gave them food for thought.

At 15.00 hours Capitaine Accart climbed for the third time into his cockpit. This time it was not a question of taking off. Three pilots of 1/5 squadron were merely taking up their action stations for a two-hour stretch. They were wearing their parachutes and helmets, with headphones and laryngophones in place. The three aircraft were lined up on the edge of the field under a camouflage net. Beside each of them stood a mechanic ready to start up the engines.

Every half an hour the engines were revved up. Time passed slowly and it was very hot. This action stations duty was always unpleasant. One either froze or fried. At 16.45 hours each of the three pilots was thinking of the appearance of his relief.

At 16.55 hours a flare went up from the squadron tent at the end of the airfield. Alert. A minute later the three aircraft taxied on to the field and took off. As soon as

Capitaine Accart was airborne he felt several violent jolts beneath his Curtiss and he saw sprays of red and black on the ground. Looking up, he caught sight of the light-coloured bellies of about thirty twin-engined German bombers. Suippes airfield was under attack.

The bombers circled at 9,000 feet above the airfield. The first thing to do was to climb up to them. Climbing in two-minute spirals which seemed incredibly long, Capitaine Accart had time to see one of the bombers crash to the ground, brought down by the French anti-aircraft. He also saw bombs hitting the nearby village.

At last he reached the height of the enemy formation. There were twenty-one Do 17s. Above them six Messerschmitts were providing air cover. At the same time as the operational patrol several Curtisses arrived from No. 2 squadron to defend the airfield.

The battle started. The Curtisses attacked the Dorniers and the Messerschmitts dived on them. Soon a dog fight was in full swing, a whirling circus of aircraft exchanging bursts in the bright blue sky. Sometimes one of the pilots yanked his stick to climb after a dive and felt glued to his seat as though his body suddenly weighed a ton. He blacked out. Close turns and violent aerobatics forced the blood to the lower part of the body, emptying the brain. For a few seconds, with eyes wide open, the pilot could see nothing. When the first flying-meeting pilots exceeded 350 m.p.h. they reported that they had experienced this sensation on turns and everyone said: "This speed will never be exceeded. The human frame will never stand up to it." But during the course of World War II the blackout was considered quite a normal incident. The fighter and bomber pilots thus became momentarily blind two or three times in almost every dog fight. They waited for it to pass, but during those seconds of blindness a certain number lost control of their machines and killed themselves.

Two Dorniers, and then a third, crashed with their engines blazing. Parachutes blossomed like white flowers. Below them the village of Suippes was almost entirely enveloped in thick black smoke shot through with gleams of scarlet flame.

Capitaine Accart had first attacked and hit a Dornier, then manoeuvred to dive on another wave of bombers and set fire to a second of the enemy. Then seeing a Curtiss being attacked by two Messerschmitts he dived to help his comrade. It seemed impossible to fight methodically in this free-for-all but Capitaine Accart thought that none of his bullets had been wasted. The problem of firing in the air is extremely complicated. The single-seater fighter is normally armed with a fixed weapon firing ahead in the axis of the aircraft. The enemy's approach angle as well as his speed and distance must be calculated; taking these factors into account the pilot must aim a certain distance ahead or to stern of the target. These appreciations and corrections, as well as the pointing of the aircraft, have to be made in a flash, one might almost say by instinct.

Capitaine Accart felt surprised and somewhat bewildered when he noticed that there were no more German aircraft over the airfield. The Messerschmitts were now several miles to the west in a dog fight with a few Curtisses. The surviving Dorniers had set an easterly course and were re-grouping as best they could. Capitaine Accart saw a straggler within reach and dived on him.

His ammunition was not yet exhausted and he could now fight methodically. He gave the Dornier a long burst. Increasing his speed, he drew so close that he could see the holes of the bullets he had just fired in the metal of the aircraft. He began to press his firing button and to aim at the cabin. All his bullets found their mark. Suddenly he broke off his fire. One of the bomber crew had baled out. The parachute opened.

The French captain continued to escort the Dornier at a short distance, ready to resume fire but without actually firing. It was at this moment, as he himself said, that he felt "more upset than I have ever been in my life."

A member of the crew had jumped from the rear bomb bay but his parachute had opened immediately, that is to say, too soon, and had got caught in the fuselage. The unfortunate man tugged at his liftwebs, trying without success to climb back into the aircraft. Capitaine Accart continued to fly quite close to the Dornier, wondering what the pilot was going to do and whether he ought to start firing again to force him down. The man on his parachute was still struggling desperately. At last the pilot baled out and his parachute opened. The bomber went into a dive. With the increasing speed the entangled man was slowly dragged back towards the tail and glued to the fuselage. The engines were still revving and the bomber dived more steeply, finally crashing with a formidable explosion.

The Messerschmitts had reformed 1,500 feet above him and returned to escort the bombers. Accart, however, had time to attack a second Dornier and to set fire to one of its engines. Another Curtiss dispatched this aircraft while the Capitaine returned to Suippes since he had no ammunition left.

The runway was dotted with bomb craters. By luck, none of the aircraft of 1/5 which had remained on the ground had been hit. Eight German twin-engined machines had been shot down. The village of Suippes had suffered a terrible ordeal: 47 dead and 100 wounded. "Mutilated women and children lay in a long row; it was a pathetic sight," wrote Capitaine Accart. "No, a thousand times no, war is a monstrosity."

Apart from the eight bombers, the 1/5 group (first and second squadrons of No. 5 wing C.O. Commandant Murtin) had shot down three Me 110s. Violent dog fights took place over nearly all the north-eastern air front. Forty-nine German planes (37 confirmed) were destroyed. Four French pilots were killed, five wounded and five had baled out and landed safely.

On the following day, the 11th May, there was a rumour that the Germans had taken three bridges over the Albert Canal before the Allies had had time to blow them up. German armour was streaming across. The cavalry of the Second Army continued to fall back.

At 18.00 hours No. 6 bomber group received orders to attack the famous bridges to the west of Maestricht. Twelve Lioré 45s, escorted by eighteen Morane 405s, carried out the mission, delivering their attack at low altitude under very heavy flak and among a swarm of Messerschmitts. One of the bridges was damaged and one bomber was shot down. Of the eleven which returned, seven were so badly damaged that they had to be sent immediately to the repair shop.

That day the French fighter arm shot down 39 enemy aircraft (27 confirmed) and lost five of its pilots. Capitaine Accart, for his part, shot down a Heinkel 111 after an absolutely classic attack with two consecutive bursts, one in each engine. The following day at 10.00 hours he took off at the head of a double patrol composed of six Curtisses to cover French troops who were fighting a delaying action. Capitaine Accart spotted a Dornier 215 which had penetrated far behind the French lines. He dived on it until he was no more than fifty yards away. At this distance all his bullets found their mark and he could distinctly see their impact on the enemy's engine. He could also see quite distinctly the spurts of fire from the Dornier's cannon. At one moment, he almost instinctively huddled in his seat with his head stuck in his shoulders and felt a violent shock on his face.

When he came to his senses he saw the earth racing up towards him. He pulled out. Blood was trickling down his eyelids. Although he was half-blinded with blood he noticed, however, that one of his team was finishing off the Dornier.

He called over the radio to the leader of No. 2 patrol.

"Hallo, Marina. I've been hit. Take over command and complete the mission."

Then he made for Suippes and landed. His wounds were superficial; his face and eyelids had merely been scratched by splinters from his broken windscreen. As he got out of his aircraft he noticed that a bullet had grazed his helmet, broken his goggles and had burst exactly in the centre of his head cushion.

"Marina" was the code name for Lieutenant Marin La Meslée. After taking his degree in philosophy Marin la Meslée obtained his pilot's certificate in 1931 at the age of nineteen. This tough, six foot youth was only happy when he was in the air. He joined the Armée de l'Air and as a fighter pilot and Sous-Lieutenant on the Reserve he came to a decision: "I shall remain in the Army. I want to go on flying."

"You can't remain on the active list with your rank," replied the officer at the personnel bureau. "You can only rejoin as a Sergeant."

"Very well, then. I'll sign on again as a Sergeant."

Posted to the 2nd Fighter Regiment at Strasbourg, Marin la Meslée asked permission to follow the preliminary courses for Saint-Cyr at the Alsation Lycée.

"Impossible. It's against the regulations. But you can prepare yourself in your spare time."

To prepare for the entrance to a big school "in your spare time" is an illusion. Marin la Meslée was "ploughed".

In 1934 a ministerial decree authorized Lieutenants on the Reserve to "serve on the active list." Marin la Meslée wrote to the Ministère de l'Air.

"I herewith beg to apply for the cancellation of my N.C.O.'s term of service and to be confirmed in my rank of Sous-Lieutenant and to be admitted into the ranks of the Armée de l'Air on the active list." The reply arrived a few days later. "Permission refused."

"Good," said la Meslée. "I shall apply for the cadet officers' course."

He wrote once more to the Ministry and received another reply. "You cannot enter this course before completing your period of two years as a sergeant. It is useless to insist."

Marin la Meslée completed his two years as a Sergeant Pilot. Between his duties and late into the night he prepared his cadet officer's course. He was accepted and put up his Sous-Lieutenant's stripe on leaving the Ecole de l'Air on the 1st October, 1937. He had beaten the administration.

That morning of the 12th May, 1940, when Capitaine Accart handed over to him the command of the double patrol which was now reduced to five aircraft, a score of Junkers 87s had appeared over the Ardennes forest with the intention of dive-bombing concentrations of the 2nd Army cavalry. The nightmare of the French ground troops began. The fighters of 1/5 intercepted the Junkers.

These dive-bombers were slower but easier to handle than

the Curtisses. No sooner were they engaged in combat than they jettisoned their bombs to deal with their assailants. Marin la Meslée and his comrades were experienced pilots with great training in aerobatics; this had seemed useless enough in peacetime but it now proved the safeguard of the fighter pilot in battle. The ensuing dog fight lasted only a few minutes. The junkers who had not been shot down set their course at full throttle for home.

The parachutes of the German aviators who had baled out had not yet reached the trees before a second enemy formation appeared. Another violent battle ensued. More Junkers fell in flames. More parachutes unfolded. A quarter of an hour after the start of the first action the sky was clear of enemy aircraft. Twelve dive-bombers were shot down and the French patrol only lost a single pilot.

Marin la Meslée shot down two Junkers. This made three with a Do 17 reconnaissance plane shot down on the 11th January east of Verdun. That day the French fighter arm destroyed 52 enemy aircraft (32 confirmed) and lost three pilots. Six were wounded and two baled out and landed safely.

On the same day eighteen Breguet 693s from the I/54 and II/54 Groups of assault aviation attacked the enemy armoured columns in the region of Tongres in Belgium. These Breguets were two-seater monoplanes in which the pilot and the machine-gunner were back to back. The pilot used the cannon and the two front machine-guns and dropped the bombs. He had no view to the rear. The machine-gunner protected the aircraft from the rear in case of enemy fighter attack. He could see nothing of what was going on ahead. The two men communicated by telephone but the pilot had to disconnect the telephone if he wanted to speak to the ground or to another aircraft.

The Breguets carried out their attacks above the roads at tree level, bombing, machine-gunning and using their cannon on the vehicles, the hoods of which were painted bright orange to allow them to be recognized by the German planes. (The few French aircraft available could of course also recognize them!) The attack was an unqualified success. The rear gunners of the Breguets saw the debris of tankers and trucks exploding and flying into the air. But the German armoured troops did not waver under the aerial attacks: they replied with flak installed on special vehicles interspersed between every ten or twelve trucks. Hosts of bluish tracer bullets rose towards the attacking aircraft and the occupants of the Breguets heard a hail of metal rattle against their wings.

Eight Breguets out of the eighteen were shot down (seven out of eleven of Group 1/54). One of the aircraft which got back bore the traces of 250 bullets.

On the 13th May, the pilots of fighter group 1/5 (Commandant Murtin, Squadron Leaders Capitaine Accart and Lieutenant Dorance) learned that the group had been mentioned in Army dispatches as having achieved 33 dazzling victories without suffering any loss to themselves in the course of the three first days of the real war. (During the "phoney" war the Squadron had shot down six enemy machines!) The pilots of Group 1/5, in common with all their comrades on the north-eastern air front had haggard faces, drawn features and red eyes. On the ground they had only two wishes: to eat and sleep – above all, to sleep. Now it was more than ever a question of trying to get one's fill of sleep. North-west of Sédan the infantry, overwhelmed by the attacks of the dive-bombers, gave ground. "Where are *our* planes?" grumbled the soldiers.

The French planes were really very few compared with the enemy aerial fleet, but the soldiers fighting on the ground imagined that they were even less numerous or lacking altogether. The dog fights invariably took place at very high altitude, beyond their range of vision.

On the 13th May, the French High Command, in order to raise the morale of the army, ordered several fighter squadrons "to show themselves" to the troops by patrolling at 1,500 feet. Now at this altitude the French fighters could not usefully engage the enemy dive-bombers. They formed an ideal prey for Messerschmitts flying above them and they were dangerously exposed to the German flak. Nevertheless these missions were carried out in addition to real air-cover operations.

In the course of one of these, three patrols from 1/5 squadron waded into attack a formation of forty German bombers escorted by Me 109s and 110s. One of the Curtisses was set on fire and the pilot baled out. Marin la Meslée shot down two Me 109s. During their aerobatics among the gleaming tracer bullets, the pilots occasionally caught sight of a great black patch dotted with fires below them – Sédan.

Sédan was the place chosen by Hitler to pierce the French Front. A ram of more than forty divisions, ten of them armoured, raced to this point. On the 14th May, the French High Command gave the bomber arm the following orders: "Destroy the bridges over the Chiers and the Meuse above and below the town." The order carried a rider: "Mission to be carried out at all costs."

Among the few dozen bombers available were Nos. 34 and 38 Squadrons of Amiot 143s.

These machines dated from 1930 and flew at 140 m.p.h. On account of their slow speed and the absence of all armour plating which made them incredibly vulnerable, they had until then been designed for use as night bombers; for this reason they were painted entirely in black. Towards midday on the 14th May, they took off at the same time as the Lioré-Olivier 45s from Group 6 in a perfectly clear sky and brilliant sunshine. A formation of Morane 406 fighters gave air cover to the operation. The altitude laid down for the bombing was 2,500 feet. Above Sédan the fighters had to gain height to beat off attacks from superior numbers of Messerschmitts while the heavy bombers continued to advance in slow horizontal flight above the veritable forest of flak which spurted from the ground. The most impressive description of this operation was published by the German paper *Die Wehrmacht* signed by Major von Kilmansegg, G.S.O.1 of the 1st Panzer Division.

"It really needed audacity and guts to dive into the hell unleashed by our flak batteries," wrote this officer. "The enemy aircraft were shot down unceasingly. After each hit the explosion sent up a plume of flame which remained for a moment suspended vertically above the blazing inferno. Sometimes one or two white parachutes detached themselves from the lost machines and slowly descended. During the day of the 14th May, at one single point of the line the enemy lost more than forty aircraft, twenty-eight of which were shot down by the flak of the 1st Panzer Division alone."

The German account is more or less accurate. Forty aircraft were shot down above Sédan and the environs. At the end of the day three bridges had been destroyed but this hardly slowed down the enemy advance. On the morning of the 16th, the French 9th Army which had defended the crossings of the Meuse had been practically wiped out.

Fighter Squadron 1/5 was no longer stationed at Siuppes but at Saint-Dizier. On the 14th May, the Curtisses had beaten off a bomber attack directed against their airfield. Then, during the afternoon, the order to move arrived. The retreat of the aerial formations, necessitated by the German ground advance began.

"All the pilots are in a low physical and moral state," one can read in a medical report of the period. "Among them are to be found cases of instability, insomnia, encephalitis, considerable modification of arterial tension, a progressive emanciation due firstly to the great efforts demanded (numerous missions at altitude since November and a permanent state of alert since May 12th) and secondly to a physiological loss of appetite. Complete rest in proportion to their condition seems absolutely essential to enable the pilots to recover the necessary physique demanded by their missions." Instead of this absolutely essential rest they were sent on almost uninterrupted patrols to protect the Front entailing several flights a day and to furnish cover for their bombers and the Potez 63 reconnaissance aircraft.

When there was a lack of Potez 63s the fighters themselves carried out the reconnaissance missions. In the pilots' reports one finds no allusions to their low physical and moral state, only an enumeration of the missions carried out with curt technical descriptions of the battles and the number of aircraft shot down.

On the 22nd and 23rd May, 1940, Lieutenant Marin la Meslée carried out two lone reconnaissance flights over the enemy lines along a stretch of a hundred miles, hedge-hopping at 150 feet to avoid the flak. (The unexpected fighter flying at 150 feet has disappeared before the gunners have had time to aim.) He was also in several airfights in company with his squadron comrades. By the end of May, 1940, he had shot down eighteen enemy aircraft (thirteen confirmed, five probables). This honour made him the leading French ace of World War II, his squadron leader, Capitaine Accart, being a close second with fifteen victories (twelve confirmed, three probables). We quote the figures here because they are on record and figure in the tables of honour, but one must not let oneself be fascinated by this type of sporting classification. Every airman will tell you that conditions of aerial warfare have developed since the 1914–18 war and an ace is not necessarily appreciated in his own squadron, particularly if he possesses the "ace mentality", that is to say, if he wants at all costs to increase the number of his trophies.

The pilot who is appreciated is the man who is capable of team work. This means to keep his place in the formation, to watch for attacks from behind, to warn his mates of the arrival of an enemy, to go swiftly to their aid, sure of being helped himself in similar conditions. This solidarity enables the squadron to fight most effectively and with least losses.

Of course this by no means signifies that the ace must be considered *a priori* as a bad team mate; on the contrary, he may possess all the qualities of one, plus skill, a cool head and audacity which with a bit of luck will allow him to shoot down more of the enemy than the others. Two men gave very obvious proof that they possessed all these qualities: Accart and Marin la Meslée.

These two pilots were to finish the French campaign with a score of sixteen and twenty respectively. Their personal successes certainly counted less in their own eyes than the following figures: 1/5 squadron, which they alternately commanded, won a total of 71 victories at the cost of a single life as a result of enemy action (Sergeant

72

Pilot Morel killed in a fight with twenty He 111s on the 18th May, 1940; two pilots were killed as a result of passing out at high altitude; and five were seriously wounded). This admirable economy proves that the two aces were also intelligent leaders, competent, eager to procure the maximum of security for their subordinates in the extraordinarily difficult circumstances in which they were fighting.

A naval air service pilot at the beginning of his career, Jean Accart had acquired once and for all their spirit of absolute solidarity to be found among seafaring men. During the last two weeks of May, 1940, he was seen to take advantage of half a day's rest while his damaged aircraft was being repaired to jump into a car and drive to Château-Thierry. Two pilots from his squadron had not returned from a dog fight the night before over Fismes and La-Fère-en-Tardenois. Accart found one of them slightly wounded in the hospital at Villiers-sur-Marne and learned that the second, also wounded but out of danger, had been evacuated. Reassured, he returned to Suippes. On both the outward and the return journey he drove along roads encumbered by a fleeing population – broken down carts loaded with old people and household objects, children's perambulators camouflaged with branches. Bombing attacks were in progress all round them and each time the terrified flock screamed in terror. Buses full of retreating infantrymen cleaved a passage through the crowd. These pathetic pictures aroused no trace of contempt or reprobation in this flying ace. His description merely expresses a deep and very human pity. Capitaine Accart stopped and gave a lift to a woman with two babies, taking them and two nurses to the station. "I arrived at Saint-Dizier for dinner with my faith in victory shaken. For if the Aisne Front is broken we have no men or material left to resist in depth or to allow a serious regroupment on the Marne." The fruitless struggle now began.

On the 19th May, AB.2 and AB.4 Squadrons, released from the aircraft carrier *Béarn* and stationed at Berck, received orders to co-operate in delaying the German advance by attacking a concentration of armour at Berlaimont crossroads near Aulnoye on the Sambre.

These squadrons, commanded respectively by Lts. Lorenzi and Laine, were equipped with Loiré-Nieuport 411 single-seater dive-bombers. The word dive-bomber usually conjures up a picture of terrifying meteors. Although the Loiré-Nieuport could reach a fine speed in a steep dive, in level flight it never exceeded 150 m.p.h. Its armament consisted of one cannon and two machine-guns; protection against enemy fire was non-existent and a machine-gun bullet fired at fifty yards could penetrate the armour-plated screen behind the pilot's seat.

Accordingly, the two squadron leaders took off without fighter cover at the head of all their available aircraft (eleven from AB.2 and nine from AB.4). The Loiré-Nieuports arrived above the German tanks, dispersed in a big field north of the village of Berlaimont. A considerable number of flak batteries were already in position and they opened fire immediately. The French aircraft dived and released their bombs.

The report of the operation maintains that although numerous German tanks were certainly destroyed it was impossible to observe the results of the attack with any degree of accuracy. A hail of flak bullets rose from the smoke of explosions, geysers of earth and flames spurting from shot-down aircraft. The losses, however, could be given accurately: ten aircraft did not return. Several of those which got home were seriously damaged.

On the following day, still without fighter cover, the three remaining airworthy machines of the two squadrons took off once more from Berck, this time in company with A.B.1 (10 Chance Voughts) led by Lieutenant Mesny, to destroy a bridge over the Oise near Origny-Sainte-Benoîte.

The formation was intercepted by a group of Messerschmitts half-way to the target. The six leading aircraft of AB.1 squadron were shot down and the others dispersed.

Luckily the Messerschmitts did not spot the three Loiré Nieuports, which flew on and eventually arrived at the target. Here, too, the flak batteries were already in position. The French aircraft attacked the bridge in a 60° dive from 3,000 feet. The bridge was cut and one of its piles collapsed. The two aircraft from AB.4 returned badly damaged. The sole surviving machine of AB.2 was shot down by the flak on the bridge.

On the 24th May, 1940, a Laté 298 seaplane left the water at Cherbourg for Dunkirk carrying mail for the admiral commanding the northern theatre of naval operations. Its crew consisted of CPO Pilot Lachney and Wireless PO Goret acting as captain and rear-gunner. The Laté 298 also had a forward machine-gun for the use of the pilot. This ancient machine flew at 100 m.p.h.

The seaplane had to follow the coast until it reached the semaphore station at Gravelines and from there to take the air channel as far as Dunkirk. It set out at 150 feet with slight northerly breeze blowing, ceiling unlimited, visibility twelve miles.

At 11.15 hours, two sea miles from the Gravelines station, the wireless captain spotted a German aircraft flying at 3,000 feet, 2,000 yards to the south-west. It was a Messerschmitt 110 (two cannon, five machine-guns, speed 356 m.p.h.). "Sparks" notified the pilot and lined up his machine-gun.

The Messerschmitt spotted the seaplane and opened fire. When it was 700 yards away Goret replied. Here is his report:

"The seaplane carried out some speedy avoiding action! Enemy aircraft made three attacks.

"During these three attacks the pilot was never in a position to fire, the difference in speed being too great. He did not fire.

"The wireless officer was the first to open fire at 700 yards.

"His loader exhausted, he changed it while the enemy aircraft broke off the action between the first and second run-ins. After a burst the machine-gun jammed. The Wireless PO could then only fire single shots. The enemy fired with all his fixed weapons.

"After a five-minute combat at two and a half miles North 70°W of Dunkirk in the course of the third attack, the seaplane, out of control, fell into the sea. It broke up and sank immediately.

"The pilot, wounded in the head, was held up in the water for ten minutes by his comrade but he sank.

"The Wireless PO managed to swim to the cargo boat *Lucien-Gougy* which was making for the scene of the air battle. He reached it after forty-five minutes.

"Searches carried out by the *Lucien-Gougy* failed to find the envelope containing the post for the Maritime Prefecture No. 1 region and the book of naval signals."

After the war an illustrious German pilot wrote the following phrase in his memoirs: "I still wonder how some of those French airmen dared to attack us with the aircraft and weapons they possessed." Perhaps it was he who brought down the Postal seaplane. One can easily imagine the German pilot appalled at seeing the rear gunner of the Laté 298 – a sitting duck as regards speed – opening fire and replying to the end, to the formidable hail of the Me 110's projectiles; and once the gun had jammed continuing to fire single shots as though with a sporting gun. I find this small episode significant, and, to a certain extent, as impressive as many of the great air battles of World War II.

On the previous night four similar seaplanes, commanded by Lt. Laniot had met nine Me 109s and opened fire on them. The airmen fighting in these Late 298s could not obviously hope to remain in the sky for more than a few minutes. One of them, however, managed to save his aircraft by slipping into a rainstorm after his gunner had been seriously wounded. The balance sheet of those few-minute combats was two dead, four missing and two wounded.

The squadrons of the Naval Air Service, retreating from base to base as the Germans advanced, were engaged until the end, particularly in actions against the harbour of Genoa and the Italian fleet. The airmen of this service were among those who fought in the worst conditions of inequality.

But let us now return to the Land Air Force.

On the 1st June, 1940, Capitaine Accart took off from

Saint-Divier airfield at the head of a patrol of three Curtisses. His mission was to intercept on the return journey a fleet of enemy bombers reported in the region of Bourges. The German raids had now extended deep into the heart of France.

Shortly after they were airborne the base radio station, which should have kept the patrol informed of the movements of the enemy formation, ceased to transmit. *Broken down again,* thought Accart. *Lucky that visibility is good and we have a chance of spotting the Boches ourselves. They should try to cross the frontier north of Basle.*

The patrol, without having seen anything, reached the Gray vertical (north east of Dijon) on the expected return route of the bombers and began to circle. Nothing in sight. A fighter aircraft cannot go on circling in the sky for hours: the endurance of a Curtiss was one hour twenty minutes.

The Saint-Dizier ground station was still out of action. Capitaine Accart was on the point of giving orders to return home when he heard a crackle in his headphones and then a strangely clear voice.

"Hallo 307. Hallo 307. Forty enemy bombers making their way up the Rhone valley south of Lyon, altitude 15,000 feet."

It was another fighter group station speaking but Accart did not know which one. The Capitaine glanced at his map and calculated rapidly. The bombers would cross the Juras. There was insufficient fuel to engage them and to get home afterwards. But there *was* time to land at Dijon, refuel and take off to intercept them.

He gave his orders and a few minutes later the three Curtisses landed at Dijon. The deserted airfield was riddled with bomb craters and the hangars were half destroyed. A few mechanics came up. They looked exhausted and their faces were gloomy.

"This station has been evacuated. We're just leaving ourselves."

"Can we at least get some fuel?" asked the Capitaine.

A fuel truck was still there. One of the Curtisses had hardly filled its tanks when the sirens began to wail.

"Take off straight away and cover the airfield," Accart

ordered the pilot of the re-serviced aircraft.

While the tanks of the other two were filled, the mechanics looked at the sky. Capitaine Accart still had to fill in and sign a few forms in the proper manner. At last the patrol was airborne.

Accart once more heard station 307 following the flight of the German bombers and ordering a patrol to make its way to Dijon at 12,000 feet. The curtisses headed for the city. Soon they could see five Dewoitine 520s below them. This machine, which had gone into service on the 15th May, could fly at 330 m.p.h. Armed with a 23 mm. cannon and four machine guns, it was the only French aircraft which could fight an Me 109 on equal terms.

Station 307 now directed the Dewoitines to Pontarlier. The Curtisses followed them. Suddenly one of the Dewoitines called base.

"I can see three single-seaters above me."

"What did you say?"

"They're probably British," said a Dewoitine pilot.

"Go and identify them but don't fire."

Accart showed his cockades to his unknown comrades.

"Hallo, 307. They're Curtisses," said the Dewoitine leader.

The Curtiss pilots heard the speakers from Station 307 questioning each other. "What group can they belong to? What are they doing here?" At that moment the German bomber formation appeared to the S.S.E. and the Curtisses and Dewoitines waded in.

Etiquette demanded that the Dewoitines, which were in their own sector, should be given the initiative for the operation. The latter approached on the tail of the bombers, attacking the centre and the right wing. Accart and his fellow pilots dived on the left wing. An He 111 loomed large in his gonio. He pressed his machine-gun button and fired several bursts. The bomber began to smoke and to lose speed. *He's had it*, though Accart. At that moment he himself fainted.

His first sensation on regaining consciousness was that of blood flowing down his face, as on the day when a bullet had smashed his windscreen. But this time his situation must be more serious for the Captain felt that he was still not entirely conscious. He was still half-dazed as though he had been felled by a blow on the head.

He examined more closely his gloved hand which he had instinctively run over his face. It was red with blood. He then noticed that it was his right hand which he normally used on the control column. His joystick was free. His left hand was still clutching the throttle which was opened full. Accart then had the idea of looking at his air-speed indicator. The needle showed 400 m.p.h. and was creeping forward on the dial. The Curtiss had far exceeded its maximum horizontal speed and was certainly in a dive.

Almost blinded by blood, he could see nothing in the narrow confined space of his cockpit. *I must try and bale out*, he thought. It cost him an enormous effort of will power to open the cabin and manoeuvre the apparatus which freed his lift webs and belts. All his movements were extraordinarily slow and the ground must be approaching at a terrifying speed. At last Accart put his left arm outside the aircraft. It was immediately blown back by the speed. With another desperate effort the Capitaine managed to fling himself into the void.

A body, as it leaves the machine, falls at the same speed as the aircraft. If the parachute opens at that moment it is instantly torn. He has to make a delayed drop to let the weight of the body have its effect. Naturally one must not wait too long. Capitaine Accart had only one good arm and his hand instinctively sought for the rip cord on his chest. Once more he fainted.

He was brought back to his senses again by some extremely painful jolts. He heard the noise of an engine – a car engine. When he opened his eyes he saw a nurse bending over him.

"Well, you're French, anyhow, eh? So much the better. You're all right, *mon vieux*. You're saved.

At Pontarlier he learnt that he had an open fracture on his left leg, broken teeth, multiple contusions and shrapnel splinters in his face. One of these splinters had penetrated half an inch deep between his two eyes without, by some miracle, touching the brain.

After an operation on his leg Capitaine Accart was evacuated to Lyon hospital.

He was transported in a small Red Cross aircraft. The pilot, a reservist, declared as night fell, that he had never done any night flying and that moreover the mist was beginning to cover the ground. The wounded man lying there, unable to see anything through his bandages, began to give him advice.

"The Ambérieu airfield is often clear when Bronne is covered, so try and land there. As you come down, keep the engine ticking over at minimum speed."

Instead of listening to his advice, the pilot cut off his engine completely. The aircraft bounced. He pushed his throttle forward again, did another circle in the dark, his wings swaying perilously.

He's going to buy it, though Accart. But luck had not abandoned the Squadron Commander of 1/5. The aircraft pancaked at last, but without any breakage. Half an hour later, Accart was once more on the operating table. The war in France was not to last long enough to allow him to return to the command of his squadron.

The new squadron commander of 1/5 was Marin la Meslée. On the 3rd June he received orders to take off with all the available aircraft of his unit to intercept a formation of German bombers on their way to Paris. Above Rheims the Curtisses met fifty Dornier 215s escorted by Messerschmitts, which they attacked head on. After a rapid engagement the German formation scuttled for home. Marin la Meslée was chasing and had already damaged a Dornier straggler when two fighters dived on him. Thinking that two of his comrades had come to give him a hand, he did not turn away from his target. He heard a terrible report and saw his windscreen and instrument panel covered with stars. His comrades, of course, were two Me 110s. Marin la Meslée was able to shake them off in a dive almost to the ground. He returned to base. On the ground he saw that the German bullets had outlined the shape of his head on the instrument panel. Not a single bullet had grazed him.

The squadron was in several more actions and shot down more enemy aircraft between the 3rd and 11th June, the day the group received orders to leave Saint-Dizier. The battle continued for another few days in extremely difficult conditions with one retreat after the other, communications growing more and more precarious and the pilots wondering at each landing if they would find the airfield already in the hands of the enemy.

On the 20th June the Curtisses of 1/5, led by Marin la Meslée, crossed the Mediterranean and landed at Algiers. At the end of the month they were disarmed according to the terms of the Armistice. Since the war started, as I have already mentioned, they had a score of 71 victories.

Other units with less victories to their credit fought under equal, if not greater difficulties. This was the case, for example, with squadron 1/2 ex-SPA 3, Guynemer's squadron.

SPA 3 (of which SPA 67, later 1/5, was as I explained above, the "daughter-in-law") had been given its new title between the two wars: Squadron 1/2. But all the airmen in it continued to call it SPA 3 and the tradition was cultivated more religiously than in any other unit.

A stork with the lowered wings was painted on all the aircraft and engraved on all the furniture. In a showcase in the pilots' mess could be seen the famous fetish – a plush, rather moth-eaten, stork. The walls were covered with photos and portraits of Guynemer and the other squadron aces. Before being accepted by his comrades, every new pilot had to read the log book of the 1914–18 war with a list of the 175 confirmed victories and 161 probables. Now, on the morning of the 3rd June, 1940, nine months after the outbreak of hostilities, SPA 3 had only one victory to its credit.

During the first five months of the war this squadron was stationed at Beauvais and its pilots had not caught a glimpse of a single German aircraft. Later the unit transferred to the eastern zone of operations and its pilots had been unlucky on the rare occasions they had been able to meet the enemy. Had they been luckier, chance would have had difficulty in overcoming the terrible material inferiority which handicapped them *vis-à-vis* their adversaries. SPA 63, heir to a fabulous tradition, was equipped with Morane 406s.

The Morane 406 flew at 280 m.p.h. and climbed at 36 feet per second. The Me 109, put into service in November, 1940, reached a speed of 330 m.p.h. and climbed at 63 feet per second. Its weapons functioned in bands on the continuous feed system, whereas the Morane 406 used loaders impossible to replace in flight and giving only 15 seconds firing time. I have already mentioned the superiority in speed of the Morane 406 over the bombers and German "recce" planes; it will be remembered that this was only about six m.p.h. When the fighter pilots of SPA 3 attacked from the rear of the German formation in the classic manner they could not plunge upon them like vultures. They pursued them with difficulty, exposed to the rear gunner's fire from the bombers and to the lightning attacks of the escorting Messerschmitts. When they broke off the action after firing they were forced to give up all hope of ever getting back to the formation.

"On the evening of the 2nd June," wrote Capitaine Williame, commanding SPA 3, "Major Darou said to me that the general commanding the eastern zone of operations was surprised that during two days' ops on the 1st and 2nd June we had not yet shot down a single machine. With tears in my eyes I replied that we could do no better. Of the three aircraft which had attacked, one had been set on fire and the other seriously damaged by the enemy fire. It was not our fault if our old-fashioned aircraft gave us no scope for manoeuvre."

The memoirs of Capitaine Robert Williame, who took over command of SPA 3 in 1937 at the age of 26, reveal the personality of a leader remarkably skilled in his profession, intelligent and benevolent, non-conformist, knowing how to expose with force and clarity the reasons for the technical and numerical inferiority of French aviation in 1939–40, but criticizing with equal severity what he considered to be his personal failings. "I was very sensitive to this reproach," he added, with reference to the interview on the 2nd June. "After thinking the matter over for a long time I had to admit that I had made a mistake. The right way would probably have been to attack from head-on slightly from below or from three-quarters to the rear in a rather steep dive."

The new method was put into practice on the 5th June against a formation of fifteen Junkers 81s. Four were shot down, two of them by Capitaine Williame. On the 8th June, SPA 3 received orders to land on Coulommiers airfield where other fighter aircraft were already concentrated with a view to making a concerted effort against the terrible activity of enemy bombing. Williame arrived with a patrol of nine aircraft.

"The sector's very bad," one of his comrades said. "This evening three of you will be missing."

The patrol duly took off. From the air they could see several cities on fire. The Morane 406s sighted and attacked a formation of twenty bombers escorted by Me 109s and 110s. Capitaine Williame shot down three enemy fighters in fifteen seconds. No airman in the world had ever performed such a feat before.

On the same day he took off again at the head of his patrol and during this second sortie shot down three Ju 87s (Stukas). Six aircraft shot down in three and a half hours was another world record. SPA 3 won nine victories that day and three on the following day. In all it was to win twenty-one plus seven probables.

From the 3rd September, 1939, to the 23rd June, 1940, the French fighter arm (less than 500 machines) shot down 1,000 German aircraft for the loss of more than 200 pilots.

We know that the fighter pilots of the R.A.F. from the 1st August onwards had to wage a long, terribly hard and ultimately victorious battle against the Luftwaffe over Great Britain. "One cannot underestimate the part played indirectly by our pilots in the British victory," wrote Air Vice-Marshal Hébrard. "What would have happened to Great Britain had Goering, at the end of August, still possessed those supplementary effectives? Although this British victory was the miracle of a great nation's will-power, do not let us forget that this miracle would never have been realized had not the French Fighter Arm in 1940 sacrificed itself for the same cause."

Before closing this chapter, let us recall the fate of its principal characters.

Capitaine Williame, with nine victories, survived the French campaign. He was killed in October, 1940, on a training flight at Salon airfield in Provence.

Four years later, on the 20th September, 1944, Commandant Marin la Meslée landed on this same Salon airfield in command of fighter group 1/5 (Champagne Group). This unit had been re-formed and trained in North Africa after the Allied landings. Equipped with American fighter-bombers, P.47 "Thunderbolts", after a few operations over Northern Italy, it was engaged in the conquest of the left bank of the Rhine. In the course of this campaign Commandant Marin la Meslée was brought down in "a hurricane of flak over Neufbrisach bridge."

As for Capitaine – today Lt. Colonel – Accart, in November, 1942, he crossed into Spain where he was interned. On his release he reached Algiers where, in January, 1944, he founded the "Berry" Group. The unit became operational at the end of April in the ranks of the R.A.F. as Squadron 345 under the orders of "Major Bernard", Jean Accart's pseudonym. It specialized in the machine-gunning or dive-bombing of ground targets. Thirteen of his pilots were shot down in the course of three missions, almost all of them by flak.

CHAPTER FIVE

WITH THE "AEROSILURATORI"

"To sink a warship you have to lie on it and drop the bomb in its smokestack."

This is how Stefano Cagna expressed himself. In July, 1940, he had been appointed an Air Marshal. This Piedmontese, born in 1900, had been chosen as companion by Umberto Maddalena on his flight over the polar ice in search of the survivors of the airship *Italia*. It will be remembered that Amundsen's aircraft had disappeared in the course of the same quest. The whole world was thrilled when Maddalena and Cagna, two ex-sailors, finally discovered the red tent of the shipwrecked men in the white immensity. They became famous overnight.

Stefano Cagna then helped his close friend Italo Balbo to organize his big formation flights: the Western Mediterranean circuit with 61 machines, transatlantic flights to Rio de Janeiro, Chicago and New York with 36 machines, which in those days were considered sensational. On the 1st August, 1940, after his promotion to Air Marshal, he led his bombers to attack south of Formentera, a British naval formation comprised of two battleships, two aircraft carriers, cruisers and numerous destroyers.

"Drop the bomb in its smokestack!" It is easy to imagine that this method leaves very little chance of survival to the one who tries it. The famous Japanese suicide pilots, the *Kamikazes*, pushed it to its final conclusion. Before them an American airman, Lieutenant John J. Powers, had formulated the idea and put it into practice in the course of the naval air war in the Pacific. He was decorated posthumously with the Congressional Medal of Honour. But Stefano Cagna was undoubtedly the inventor and originator of the idea. He was the first to work out the tactics and to apply them. It was not surprising that he never returned from the operation.

What was the result of this sacrifice? Practically nothing.

The British formation had to change course temporarily during the attack but suffered no decisive damage. This action of the 1st August, 1940, was eagerly discussed by the Italian General Air Staff. The Mediterranean is one of the most important strategic routes of the world and Italy is a pier jutting out into the middle of the sea. The Italian Air Chiefs kept their eyes turned towards what they called "Mare Nostrum". They knew that the main task of their squadrons would be to attack British warships. The following were the conclusions of the discussions which took place after Stefano Cagna's operation:

1. In normal conditions of attack it is extremely difficult to hit a ship with a bomb.
2. In the case of a direct hit the penetration power of the bomb is sufficient to cause serious damage to a non-armoured ship but is insufficient in the case of armour-plated units or those divided into many water-tight compartments.
3. Another weapon will have to be used. This must be a torpedo which can hit the vessel in its vitals (below the armour plating).

This conclusion was a little tardy. The question of the use of torpedoes had been discussed for years between the navy and the air force; it had become of a polemic nature without any solution being found. Thus Italy entered the war in 1940 without possessing a single trained squadron of torpedo-carrying aircraft.

To make matters worse, the very few torpedo-carrying aircraft in existence at this period had no torpedoes! "A few days before the declaration of war," Lieutenant di Bella reveals in his book *Un Aviatore racconta le sue battaglie*, "an important quantity of torpedoes were sold to a foreign power. Those we obtained were taken from our gun-boats and loaned to us by the navy. Before any naval combat the first recommendation we received from the commander was to keep our eyes open and not to launch the torpedo before being sure of hitting the target."

Di Bella adds that another unpardonable mistake consisted in not having given the Italian Navy aircraft carriers; "The people who said that Italy was an aircraft carrier in itself forgot the size of the Mediterranean and the restricted range of the fighter aircraft – 120 minutes to take off, reach the scene of action, fight, return and land." Any mistake or a rather prolonged combat resulted in a forced landing far from base with the probable loss of the aircraft, or a forced landing in the sea with the certain loss of the aircraft and usually of the pilot.

Furthermore, the wireless technique in the Italian Air Force was very old-fashioned. The airmen could not communicate by radio with their stations; they had to send their messages in radio telegraph and these had to be deciphered again. The same system was used for the reply, so that each exchanged lasted half an hour: in other words, the time to fly ninety miles in an ancient aircraft or 180 miles in a modern plane. This meant, of course, that communication between the aircraft and its base ceased to exist as soon as it was airborne.

On the 15th August, 1940, five planes of 278 Squadron took off to attack the Naval Base at Alexandria. They were three-engine Savoia 79s, hastily adapted to carry torpedoes. Their crews had received no preliminary training.

The organizers, or rather the improvisers, of the operation had planned it to take place at the same time as an attack by bombers. The bad weather upset their calculations and the torpedo-carrying aircraft attacked on their own at night.

The curious layout of the military port of Alexandria forced the attackers to follow a line alone which they found themselves under the concentrated fire of the defence. The five three-engine Savoias came in from west to east at low altitude to be greeted by the bright beams of fifty search-lights and the shells of hundreds of guns of all calibre. The British and the Egyptians present at the attack exclaimed "They're mad!"

Two of the five aircraft which had been unable to drop their torpedoes on the first run circled and started again. All the torpedoes stuck in the mud except one; this damaged a French warship which the English had placed at the end of the mooring line just behind the booms. One of the aircraft was shot down.

The subsequent operations were slightly less improvised. From September, 1940, to Spring, 1941, the torpedo-carrying aircraft (Aerosiluratori) attacked British naval formations and escorted convoys in the Mediterranean, sinking the cruiser *Southampton* and the destroyer *Gallant*, and damaging the aircraft carrier *Illustrious* and the battleship *Malaya*. The *Illustrious*, hit on several occasions, finally had to spend a year in the American naval dockyard. These losses would probably have put the British fleet in difficulties had the Italian fleet intervened vigorously at that time, but it did nothing.

On the 22nd July, 1941, about midday, news reached Rome that a British naval force, which had presumbaly left Gibraltar, was north of the African coast sailing east. The information was confirmed at 19.00 hours by another message from a reconnaisance aircraft. This task force, sighted ninety miles north of Bougie, consisted of an aircraft carrier, a battleship, seven cruisers and several destroyers. It was sailing on a course S.70°E at a speed of 22 knots. The fighters from the carrier were airborne. (It was learned later that the aircraft carrier was the *Ark Royal*, the battleship the *Nelson*, and that the cruisers were the *Southampton*, *Leander* and *Liverpool*.) A third message stated that cargo ships, transports and tankers were following the naval force. They were sailing at reduced speed in order not to penetrate the zone of action of the Italian Air Force before nightfall.

At 19.30 hours, No. 283 Squadron of torpedo-carrying aircraft took off from Elmas, the main airfield of Sardinia, to attack the enemy. It consisted of nine S.79s, formed into three patrols, commanded respectively by Captain Georgio Grossi, the squadron commander, Lieutenant Pandolfi, and Captain Mojoli.

The squadron arrived at the spot indicated by the information. It saw nothing but an expanse of bare sea, turned back and landed at Elmas at 22.30 hours.

The next day, at 6.30 hours, the convoy was once more sighted ten miles west of Cap de Fer (in the waters of Bône,

Algeria). The cargo ships had joined the warships. The presence of a second battleship, the *Renown*, was reported.

At 07.00 hours General Vespignani, Air Commander of Sardinia, telephoned to Captain Grossi. His orders were: "Take off at eight o'clock. Grossi's patrol will attack the battleships; Mojoli will attack the carrier; Pandolfi will look after the cruisers, the cargo boats and the tankers."

Grossi replied: "I ask permission to attack the most vulnerable ships according to the formation of the convoy with the combined squadron."

"No," replied the General. "The orders from Rome are final."

"We shall do our best," replied Grossi.

All the airmen were fully aware of the difficulty of the task and the risks involved. Engines were started, at 07.55 hours the crews made their way across the airfield, and at 08.00 hours the nine machines were airborne.

The squadron passed over Montserrat to pick up the fighter escort provided by the operation orders and then turned on a south-south-westerly course in search of the enemy. After about an hour's flying the fighters, which had reached the limit of their range, dipped their wings in farewell and turned back. At nine o'clock the "Aerosiluratori" saw the first enemy smoke on the horizon.

The air-sea battle of the 23rd July, 1941, afterwards known as the first battle of Galita (this island is about 24 miles north of Cap Ferrat, Tunisia) has been described by Major di Bella, who took part in the action.

As soon as they caught sight of the smokestacks, the torpedo-carriers lost height and continued their flight at ten feet above the waves in order to be less visible. But almost immediately enormous geysers of water spouted from the sea all round them. The British radar had detected them and the big guns had opened fire. The pilots only just managed to avoid these columns of water which would have broken the wings of their aircraft. The terrific displacement of air shook them and they had to climb to 120 feet.

The convoy soon appeared ahead of them in all its

majesty. Big plumes of black smoke rose from the ships as they put on speed before the attack. The towering mass of the *Ark Royal* dominated the scene.

The squadron flew another few minutes in formation, then the three patrols diverged, each making for their appointed targets.

To have some idea of an action such as the one that follows one must remember that an escorted convoy does not look like a regiment on the sea in close formation. The ships are about 800 yards or more apart so that they have room to manoeuvre and avoid torpedoes. An attack taking place at the end of a convoy spread out over miles might pass unnoticed by the ships at the other end of the convoy, except as a distant action. At the outset the attacking aircraft saw their targets as little model ships spaced out at great distances on the sea, but which grew larger as they dived on their targets. Here is a bird's-eye view from di Bella's account.

"The merchant ships in this convoy sailed in three lines, each one protected by a warship. Moreover, the flanks of the convoy were defended by small ships with tremendous anti-aircraft armament. When their 'Chicago pianos' fired a burst we could see a circle of fire. Despite this firing and the close explosions of the shells, we pressed on.

"Pandolfi, Cipriani and I (Patrol No. 3) chose the centre line and slipped between the ships to go into the attack. We flew very low and as we approached the inner file the volume of firing diminished. I wondered why this was so. Perhaps the ships were waiting to get a closer look at me before intensifying their fire. But no, there was another reason I had not thought of. Ships firing point-blank inwards in convoy would have hit each other.

"Pandolfi was half a mile ahead of me and Cipriano about six hundred yards. As we approached the centre Cipriano suddenly climbed, did a steep turn and launched his torpedo against a cargo ship. Then he quickly brought his aircraft back to water level, slipped between two ships and left the convoy.

"After a few seconds his torpedo hit the vessel, which blew up. It must have been loaded with ammunition.

The explosion was so violent that the blast shook us dangerously, flinging our aircraft from side to side. A column of smoke rose more than three hundred feet in the air.

"A moment later Pandolfi launched his torpedo against a cruiser, which he hit. But I realized that he, too, had been hit.

"I myself, having drawn level with the aircraft carrier, decided to attack it. I pulled back the stick, climbed to 200 feet, and when I arrived at the aiming angle I waited to be at the right distance before launching. At this moment a destroyer and a corvette which were between myself and the aircraft carrier opened such an infernal fire on me that had I not returned to water level they would have sent me to kingdom-come before I could have launched my torpedo.

"By manoeuvring between the two warships I spotted a big cargo boat which was less well defended and a better target. I got into position. The second pilot removed the safety catch from the torpedo, waiting for my orders. I was still a little far away: 1,500 yards. The fire from the warships was still very intense.

"On reaching the best distance – 800 yards – I gave the orders to release. The aircraft bounded a little as the torpedo left. It was lighter by a ton. I was so near the cargo boat against which I had fired that I had no time to turn. I hopped over the ship, banked violently and returned to water level to avoid the bullets.

"This manoeuvre brought me right up against the aircraft carrier, so near that I almost grazed it with my wings without being hit by its fire. The Ark Royal was a gigantic vessel of more than 22,000 tons and 87 feet high. When I grazed it with my left wing I thought for the moment that I was flying past the first storey of a skyscraper. Its length never seemed to finish – 729 feet.

"As soon as I had passed the carrier I had to cross an artillery barrage. I zig-zagged and kept changing my altitude so as not to be boxed.

"At last, leaving the convoy zone of fire, I joined Pandolfi, whose aircraft was losing fuel. I took up my position on his right and signalled to him to make for North Africa, ten minutes flight away, instead of for Sardinia. As he kept losing speed I had to leave him and, a little later, I saw that he had landed in the sea. I took the bearing and sent an S.O.S. asking for a rescue seaplane. I remained for ten minutes on the spot and then made for home."

When he landed, Squadron Commander Grossi congratulated di Bella and Cipriani. His own patrol had been unable to deliver its attack because it had been broken up by British fighters. The torpedo-carrying aircraft had to attack without cover and the action had taken place outside the radius of the Italian fighters. The *Ark Royal* on the other hand constantly maintained in the air ten aircraft piloted by the best fighter pilots of the Fleet Air Arm. The aircraft of Grossi's patrol had been hit and the crews slightly wounded. Pandolfi and his crew had been taken prisoner by the British.

A few hours later, General Vespignani ordered Grossi to attack again without waiting for nightfall. Grossi told him that a new attack in these conditions would be running great risks with very little chance of success. The order was not cancelled. Only four aircraft were available. Cipriani and di Bella tossed a coin as to who should leave. Cipriani won; that is to say, he left.

Only two machines returned from the operation, and Grossi climbed out of his covered with blood.

"They wanted to send us into the attack at all costs and we were massacred," he declared. "Dollfus was shot down in the sea and is dead. Cipriani was forced to land in the sea off Cape Carbonara."

Di Bella took off immediately to go in search of his comrade. When he arrived on the spot he found nothing but a huge patch of oil on the sea. The aircraft had sunk. Fortunately, a little further off he discovered Cipriani and his crew in their little rubber dinghy. He sent an S.O.S. for a rescue seaplane and the shipwrecked airmen were picked up.

The Hurricanes and Spitfires of the *Ark Royal* had wreaked havoc among the torpedo carrying aircraft of No.

283 Squadron. During the day the unit had lost three machines and three others were out of action.

Meanwhile, the British convoy continued on its route to the east. It was attacked once more by "Aerosiluratori" from Sicily on the longitude of Cape Bon, Captain Magagnoli and Lieutenant Robone registered direct hits on two vessels. The naval aircraft attacked in turn during the night and also hit two vessels.

Cipriani, di Bella and Robone were mentioned in dispatches and received the Silver Military Medal for valour.

In a report of Task Force H dated 4th August, 1941 (published in London on the 10th August, 1948) Admiral Somerville gave the losses suffered by the convoy as follows:

"The destroyer *Fearless* torpedoed and sunk on the morning of the 23rd by an Italian torpedo-carrying aircraft with heavy casualties; light damage to another destroyer, light damage to a cruiser and a transport ship damaged."

In every country in wartime the women like to be seen with men in officer's uniform. Naturally this applied to the pretty Italian girls who went out with them to the Café Torino in Cagliari in September, 1941. On the 24th of this month the conversations were particularly animated in this particular café.

The subject of conversation, of course, was the convoy – a British convoy which, it was reported, had just left Gibraltar.

"Apparently it's the biggest one the British have ever assembled. Will the fleet try to stop it? But of course you pilots are going to attack it? It's rumoured that you're going to."

"Probably," replied the airmen.

"And when do you leave? Tonight? *Dio mio*, perhaps it will be tonight while we are asleep."

"Perhaps."

The airmen of No. 130 Aerosiluratori group stationed at nearby Elmas who had received orders to be ready for ops after midnight probably avoided answering these questions in too much detail. It was easy to see that the people who questioned them knew almost as much as they did about the famous convoy. The civilians also knew that aircraft loaded with torpedoes had just arrived at Elmas. Military secrets do not remain a secret very long in the neighbourhood of ports or air bases, whether it be in Italy or elsewhere.

The pilots received no new orders that night but on the following day the news was confirmed. The convoy had left Gibraltar and consisted of two battleships, two aircraft carriers, a number of cruisers and destroyers, plus numerous merchant ships, transport and tankers. That evening, torpedo-carrying aircraft arrived as reinforcements from the training groups and also from a group on Sicily. The officers of No. 130 group, placed under the orders of Grossi, learned that one unit would take part in the attack – the 36th Stormo, commanded by Colonel Seidl (an Italian despite his German name) which for a short time had been stationed at Decimomannu (Sardinia). Squadrons of bombers and fighters were also to take part in the operation. The convoy would be attacked in the waters off Galita Island, which it was due to pass on the 27th.

However, on the 26th December at 22.00 hours Elmas airfield was bombed by British aircraft and several of the Italian planes were damaged on the ground. Throughout the night the enemy aircraft flew over the aerodrome dropping delayed action bombs. Even if the Italian High Command had learned of the sailing of the convoy the British Intelligence Service knew perfectly well where its attackers were to be found. In daylight, the Italian airmen who had remained up all night had to inspect the airfield, find and immunize the delayed action bombs. Specialists finally got the runways in order within a few hours and repaired the damaged machines.

At 08.10 hours the reconnaissance aircraft reported that the convoy was at Long. 8° E, Lat. 37° 4' N. sailing in an easterly direction. It now included, apart from the merchant ships, and tankers, the battleships *Nelson*, *Renown* and *Prince of Wales*, and the aircraft carrier *Ark Royal*, plus a number of cruisers and destroyers.

At 09.30 hours General Vespignani telephoned to Grossi.

"Here are your orders. You will lead No. 283 Squadron and attack the aircraft carrier. Captain Melley's squadron* and Marino Marini's† will each attack a battleship. The third battleship and the cruisers will be the targets of No. 36 Stormo which will take off from Decimomannu a few minutes after you."

"I should have preferred to be left free to attack whatever proved the best target," said Grossi. "May I be allowed to remind you that a rigid allocation of targets brought useless sacrifices in July?"

This observation was of some value and Grossi was quite right to utter it in his role as commanding officer of a unit. Once more Vespignani replied that the orders from Rome were final.

"Besides," he added, "after the torpedo attack our fleet will engage the enemy naval forces with its big guns."

Unable to believe his ears, Grossi made him repeat this information.

"So the fleet is already on the way?" he asked.

"Yes, this time the sacrifice demanded of the torpedo-carrying aircraft will not be in vain. It will allow the fleet to carry out a big killing."

The aircraft from Elmas took off at 11.50 hours. The weather was favourable for surprise attack, misty and cloudy with intermittent rain.

The airmen scanned the expanse of the ocean in the hope of seeing the Italian fleet making its way to the enemy, but in vain. There was no sign.

"As usual, when it smelt a whiff of powder it turned tail and gained one of the numerous friendly ports of the mainland at full speed," writes di Bella. "We drew into closer formation to comment on this absence. We were very worried about the men coming from Decimomannu. Being much further to the west, they were unaware that the Italian fleet had put about and that they would be sacrificing themselves to open a breach for it in vain. We were

---

* Commanding No. 280 Squadron. The 130 Aerosiluratori group consisted of two squadrons, No. 283 and 280.

† In command of a unit which had come from Sicily.

quite disgusted but we continued for the honour of our service."

To discuss the reasons why the Italian fleet on several occasions avoided battle in this way would be outside the scope of this book. This navy had been built with a view to an eventual fight with the French fleet, the fleet of another Mediterranean power; but the turn of hostilities had confronted it with the British Mediterranean fleet which was greatly superior in quantity and quality: larger warships, better armed with bigger guns, better equipped with range finders and radio, and finally possessing a more competent and better trained personnel who had inherited a tradition unique in the world. Moreover, the absence of aircraft carriers was a very great handicap for the Italian fleet. Nevertheless, it fought on several occasions. Italian sailors, particularly in submarines and other light units, carried out during the course of the war extraordinarily rash exploits, making it odious to criticize the whole. On this subject we have the words of airmen to show the nature of their feelings and in what moral condition they went into battle. This evidence cannot be denied. But to return to di Bella's account.

"A strong southerly wind blew the clouds away to the north. Unfortunately, therefore, we had to attack to the south in a clear sky. The two other formations – those of Mario Marini and Franco Melley – were luckier, being able to hide themselves in the clouds for several minutes. waiting for the ships and to make a surprise attack. They dived from the clouds and attacked, seriously damaging two cruisers and registering a direct hit on the aircraft carrier. One of the torpedoed cruisers was abandoned by its crew.

"We airmen of No. 283 Squadron made several attempts to penetrate the convoy but we were unsuccessful because of the violent barrage and tough combats with enemy fighters. We were driven southwards until we almost reached the African coast."

Grossi made several more attempts to penetrate the convoy with his unit but he was again unsuccessful. His aircraft were constantly picked up by the British radar and singled out as soon as they approached. British fighters intercepted them on the return journey to Sardinia. Many members of the crews of these aircraft were seriously wounded.

The pilots of No. 283 Squadron landed on Elmas airfield "rather displeased with themselves at having failed to carry out their mission." They immediately learned that one of the planes from Sicily had been shot down. "A few moments later we were informed that the planes from Decimomannu had gone to their death and that survivors were very few."

The 36th Stormo had in fact delivered its attack with great resolution despite ack-ack fire and British fighters. Its action of the 27th September, 1941, remains one of the air-sea exploits of the war. It is only right to say a few words here of its leader.

Riccardo Emo Seidl, born in Naples in 1904, looked more like a man of the north than a Neapolitan: thoughtful, calm and silent. Joining the Navy as a volunteer and becoming midshipman in 1925, he had originally chosen a service very far removed from aviation – submarines. He was interested in torpedoes. After thirty-three months of submarines his real vocation emerged. He became observer and then pilot in the Naval Air Service. He returned to the deck of a ship once more as air chief of staff in the *Alberto di Guissano*, and then in the cruiser *Trieste*. The day there was an attempt at a catapult launching from this vessel, he was the first volunteer. His subordinates knew that he was always eager to be the first to take any risk and for this reason among others they loved and admired him.

At the end of 1933 Seidl left ships once more for aircraft. He commanded a fighter and then a naval bombing squadron. He received his baptism of fire in the Spanish War, during which he shot down six aircraft. When, in 1940, as a result of the German alliance, Italy entered the war, General Foucher appointed him his G.S.O.2. Promoted shortly afterwards to Colonel, Seidl took over command of the 36th Stormo torpedo-carrying aircraft. This unit, already nicknamed "Suicide Stormo," distinguished itself in Tunis and in Maltese waters and intervened "with great courage" in the Battle of Punta Stilo (which the British called the Battle of Calabria: 19th July, 1940). In six months of war it lost a third of its effective. The 36th Stormo received the Gold Medal for Military Valour with a dazzling citation.

Colonel Seidl, with his calm enthusiasm and also with the resources of his experience and intelligence, immediately devoted himself to perfecting the tactics and training of his unit.

The airmen of 36th Stormo were then flying a new type machine, the Savoia 84, which had an appalling reputation. It was very flabby, replied lazily to the controls, had a very short range and a really abominable engine, the Piaggio. Its worst weakness lay in its hydraulic control system, a very convenient novelty but extremely vulnerable. A single bullet could cause a leak in the thin system of tubes and the pilot then saw his undercarriage descend or his wing flaps lower unwittingly. Several of these aircraft were lost with their crews as a result of incidents of this type. None of the squadrons wanted to entertain the Savoia 84; they all preferred the old but glorious S.79 known as the "Evil Hunchback," a very handy aircraft with first-class Alfa Romeo engines.

Riccardo Seidl would have also preferred S79s for his airmen but he probably thought that, in the circumstances, it was better to get used to the material available and that courage and resolution would always carry them through. On the 16th September, 1941, when the 36th Stormo was transferred from the Italian mainland to Sardinia, Seidl travelled via Rome and promised his leaders that his group would prove the faith and mettle of Italian aviators.

The 36th Stormo, eleven aircraft in all, left for the attack in two formations, one under the direct command of Seidl, the other under the orders of Major Arduino Buri. Of the eleven aircraft, six, including that of the Colonel, did not return. There was only one survivor (picked up and taken prisoner) from the crews (thirty-five men) of the lost aircraft. As a result of the terrible casualties suffered by the Italian crews, the participation of 36th Stormo in the battle of the 27th September, 1941, has had to be reconstituted almost exclusively from British sources. Here is the testimony of a war correspondent in the *Ark Royal*.

"At last we saw what we expected to see – the wake of torpedoes making for the ship. Through my binoculars I saw the Italian aircraft gain height and fly off after making their attack. One of them passed too near a cruiser: I saw a red gleam; the shell hit the aircraft which exploded in the air. A column of smoke a hundred feet high marked the place where the aircraft had been shot down in pieces.

"Two minutes later a second wave arrived, this time directed against the flank of our convoy. An Italian pilot passing through our cross fire got into position for a run in. I saw the black torpedo fall into the water like a plummet. A column of water rose from the side of the *Nelson* which a few minutes later announced that it was hit. The aircraft was not more than 500 yards away from us and we shot it down with a well-aimed shot: I heard a voice shout: 'Another aircraft to starboard.' And in fact another Italian torpedo carrier was bearing down on us, manoeuvring for position. Caught in a box barrage it was hit immediately. It continued to fly on for some yards and then burst into a sheet of flame."

Another war correspondent gives further details. He mentions in particular the loss of a destroyer. (This was never announced by the Admiralty.)

"While the naval artillery opened fire, an officer announced: 'There are four torpedo-carrying aircraft.' One of them attacked a destroyer which immediately blew up. The fighters took off from the *Ark Royal* and engaged the enemy. A second Italian attack was organized at surprising speed. Four or five shadows sped towards us low on the water through a terrible barrage. The smoke produced by our artillery dispersed and we saw an aircraft diving towards the *Nelson*. A column of water rose against the flanks of the battleship. The aircraft was hit almost immediately by the fire of other ships and crashed into the sea."

The formation which had attacked the *Nelson* was that of Major Buri. Several of his machines were shot down during the approach so that in the final attack there were only two – the Major's and one more. According to the account of another eye witness – a naval officer on board the Nelson – it seems certain that the two aircraft launched at the same time and that the one who was shot down was not the one whose torpedo hit the battleship but the other. It was Major Buri who hit the Nelson and who returned from the operation. This is how the British officer described his attack. "His plan was obviously to launch his torpedo against the Nelson and with great resolution and courage he crossed the barrage from the other ships. He dropped his torpedo with great precision just in front of the battleship and from a short distance. The weaving warships offered him a very difficult target but the torpedo fell just ahead and hit the Nelson in the bows. Another torpedo (from the shot down aircraft) passed at close quarters to port.

"The pilot then flew very close to the Nelson, so close, in fact, that he was a difficult target against which it was almost impossible to fire. From the anti-aircraft control room I could see inside his machine. He passed below the poop of the ship and I think we all wished that such a man could go on living to fight again. The Nelson returned to Gibraltar and was out of commission for six months."

The British battleship had a hole torn in her twelve feet by fifteen. On that day, the 27th September, the Italian "Aerosiluratori" launched twenty-two torpedoes. Apart from the Nelson, the Ark Royal and several other ships were hit. The Italian fleet had certainly lost a fine opportunity of intervening.

The pilots of the Grossi group (130 Group), disappointed at not having been able to carry out their mission, asked permission to leave again for the attack as soon as they landed. Rome gave this permission at 16.30 hours.

"At 17.30 hours," di Bella tells us, "we took off with five machines and set course for Zembra. At 19.45 hours we picked up the convoy position, 10° 30′ East, 37° 20′ North and attacked it.

"I had no luck. Due to a mechanical fault my torpedo did not fall. After several attempts I had to return home.

The attack was well timed in the twilight. The other crews sank a cruiser and damaged another."

Di Bella was to take his revenge on several other occasions. He won several decorations and was promoted Major. Aduina Buri took over command of 36th Stormo, or rather its remains, with the mission of the reforming of the unit. He, too, was several times cited and decorated.

As for Colonel Seidl, who was killed in the attack, he received posthumously the Gold Medal for Military Valour. Only 85 of these decorations were given during the course of the Second World War. Of these, only four have survived the war and they are all badly mutilated.

The name of one of these holders of the Medaglia d'Oro del Valore Militare is famous in Italy. It was won by the airman Buscaglia who was considered to be his country's leading ace.

In August, 1942, Carlo Emmanuele Buscaglia was the picture of the glorious Italian airman as we like to imagine him: a dark, handsome man in a flamboyant uniform. He was 27 and the youngest "Maggiore" in the Italian Air Force. He wore six silver medals and the Iron Cross of the second class. In thirty actions, piloting a torpedo-carrying aircraft, twenty-six of his torpedoes found their mark, sinking two heavy cruisers, two auxiliary cruisers, six transports and cargo boats and damaging two battleships, an aircraft carrier, six cruisers, two destroyers and four transports. His father, Ercole Buscaglia, a man who had won two decorations in the 1914-18 war, could be very proud of such an heir. Some journalists interviewed Carlo Emmanuele, asking him questions about his career and his exploits.

"As a child Buscaglia was obstinate, proud and presumptuous. One cannot say that none of these characteristics remained but on reaching man's estate their counterparts appeared: energy and strength of character. He was a man who always went into things to the end whether it were a case of examinations, sporting or military exploits. He could be silent for now that he had scope for action he had no reason to speak.

"He was born at Novara on the 22nd September, 1915.

Originally he intended to be a lawyer but then he entered the Orioni Royal Aeronautical School. A Lieutenant Pilot, promoted Captain, and then Major for his war services, he commanded in succession No. 281 Squadron and No. 132 Aerosiluratori Group which he led to various actions, personally sinking or damaging nearly thirty enemy units. On the 28th December, 1951, on his return from operations, 126 bullet holes were found in his Savoia 79, not to mention a great rent in one wing.

"Simple, stocky and energetic in his mannerisms, Major Buscaglia replied to our questions in a resonant, occasionally rather surprised or contemptuous voice in which his Piedmontese accent could be recognized. He described his flight at wave level in the beams of the searchlights during the attack on Alexandria on the 15th August, 1940, when he hit a battleship. He explained to us the manoeuvres for launching with the aid of a little miniature silver torpedo which he always carried about with him. We also made him describe an action against an enemy Malta-bound convoy, with the explosion of a vessel carrying ammunition hit by one of his torpedoes. But the Major preferred to discuss other aspects of his life as a pilot. He spoke to us of the beauty of night flying under a host of stars when the pale moonlight casts a veil of enchantment over everything. Buscaglia possesses an innate sense of direction which often guides him better than a compass. He spoke to us, too, of his birthplace to which he is very attached, of the Novara girls which he compares with those of Turin and the girls of the south. . . . "

Handsome, brave, brilliant and happy: how many women must have smiled at him. One of his early commanders said of him:

"That fellow goes under the muzzles of the British guns as though they were firing corks."

One of his comrades insisted that Carlo Emmanuele had always nursed the ambition of sinking an aircraft carrier single-handed. He was obsessed by this idea and it made him lose his sleep. However, no one ever appeared more calm and even indifferent than Buscaglia at the moment of attack and in action. His *sang-froid* made a great impression on his crew and gave it confidence.

Before the attack, Carlo Emmanuele merely made the sign of the cross.

He expressed his own concept of battle in an article published in the review, *Ali di Guerra* on the 10th October, 1942.

"During an attack the leader must be, so to speak, more than human. He must not bother about the enemy's anti-aircraft fire or the enemy fighters. He must neglect all factors which could bring about the destruction of his aircraft and cause the death of his crew. He must keep only one thing in view – the objective he has decided to attack. Until the torpedo has been dropped at low altitude and at close quarters he must not take his eyes off the enemy unit.

"Once the mission is accomplished a new feeling takes hold of the leader – the will to save his comrades and himself and bring back to base not only the aircraft and its precious human cargo but the news of victory."

A month later the Allies landed in North Africa. On the 11th November, 1942, Buscaglia returned to base bringing back the news of another victory. He had just sunk a 10,000-ton merchant ship during an attack on a convoy which had left Gibraltar for Bougie. His "precious human cargo" was almost intact. Only the photographer Maiore was slightly wounded by a machine-gun bullet. Buscaglia himself drove him to hospital. The following day, when he learned that his C.O. was going to make a second attack on the enemy shipping now moored in Bougie Bay, Maiore asked whether he could go too. Buscaglia shrugged his shoulders and said: "You can't go into attack wearing bandages."

"They don't bother me," replied Maiore, "I can do my job all right."

Buscaglia finally gave way. Six torpedo-carrying aircraft of No. 132 group took off from the Sicilian airfield of Castelvetrano on the 12th November, 1942, at 11.45 hours.

The Bay of Bougie was full of troop transports and cargo vessels protected by cruisers and destroyers. Nearly all the ships were flying the American flag. The Italians met with an intense cannon and machine-gun fire and American fighters dived on them. Buscaglia's comrades saw that their Chief's aircraft, which had just dropped its torpedo, was being attacked by several fighters at the same time and had not broken off the engagement. They thought that one of these assailants was shot down but the Major's aircraft had a long trail of black smoke coming from it. The others lost sight of it. Buscaglia did not return.

The whole Italian Air Force was in mourning as a result of his disappearance. The pilots of No. 132 group decided that in future their unit should be called the Buscaglia group. The machines and the airmen wore an emblem which the Major himself had designed representing a knight riding a winged horse, plunging his lance into the body of an enormous marine monster.

During March, 1943, the sensational news ran through Italy that the man whom they had mourned as a dead hero was alive. He was a prisoner lying dangerously wounded in an Algiers hospital. The B.B.C. had just announced it. The Italian High Command immediately awarded Buscaglia the highest possible decoration, the Medaglia d'Oro del Valore Militare.

Alive and as prisoner, Buscaglia by no means lost his halo of glory. His prestige persisted to such good effect that when Italy was split into two factions, one fighting for the King and the other for Mussolini, the Aerosiluratori of the north and the south both claimed him: there were two Buscaglia groups.

But let Carlo Emmanuele Buscaglia give his own account of his mission and his nineteen months odyssey after taking off from Castelvetrano on the 25th June, 1944. Here are some extracts from his report:

"At 14.30 hours we arrived over the target. I launched my torpedo against an enemy vessel and machine-gunned the decks of other vessels.

"I could not observe the results. At that moment I found myself cut off. The five other aircraft for some reason had turned back and I could see them about two miles away.

"A large formation of Spitfires (I counted more than seven) pounced on me and I had to accept combat. My rear gunner and wireless operator were killed immediately. The rear machine-guns were out of action and my aircraft was set on fire.

"Enveloped in flames, my Savoia dived into the water from 200 to 250 feet. I was unconscious and I do not know how I managed to float. Maiore the photographer was near me and the others were burning in the water. Two hours later Maiore and I were picked up by a British warship. We remained unattended all the evening, that night and the following morning.

"Then we were transported to a French hospital in the Bougie zone. My companion's condition was very serious. I personally had serious burns on the feet, legs, hands, arms and face. I was blind for nearly a month.

"On the 15th November we were transported to a British military hospital near Bougie. On the 27th November Maiore died after appalling suffering.

"After the first days the British treated me a little better. On the 28th November I was transferred to another British hospital where I received excellent attention and was operated on by a famous surgeon.

"In this hospital I was questioned by an American officer of the Supreme Allied Staff on the situation of Italian aviation, Italy's war aims and my political and military ideas. I replied that as a prisoner of war I could give no information to the enemy."

The British finally handed their prisoner over to the Americans who sent him to New York. From there he was sent to a series of prisoner of war camps. Months passed. A whole year and more. The prisoners followed the progress of the war from this distant land as best they could. In Montecello Camp, Arkansas, Buscaglia took a decision the result of which no one could foresee.

"On the 14th April, 1944, as an Italian officer voluntarily collaborating with the Allied forces, I was transferred to the 1st Italian Sapper Regiment at Sutton Camp, North Carolina. . . ."

On the 27th June, this news which was almost as

sensational as the news of his disappearance had been spread through Italy. The Americans had repatriated him by air. He had presented himself to the Allied Commission for Aviation at Bari and had been transferred to the Italian military authorities.

That evening Buscaglia learned that he had been posted to the 28th Aviation Group at Campo Vesuviano: with rank of Major. What an extraordinary feeling after such an interlude!

The airmen of No. 28 Group flew Baltimores provided by UNRRA. This civilian relief organization for the liberated countries obviously did not give the combatants who had joined in the fight against the Third Reich the best of allied material. On the 24th August, 1944, Buscaglia took off solo in a Baltimore which the pilots of No. 28 Group had so far used as a duel-control machine. The airfield stretched to the foot of Vesuvius between vineyards turning gold in the rays of the sun. They saw the aircraft taxi become airborne against a brilliant blue sky, then suddenly stall and crash.

Thus ended the career of Carlo Emmanuele Buscaglia, the glorious, brilliant, carefree aviator who had later been an unfortunate wounded man transported from one hospital to another, then a homesick prisoner who must have suffered when he had to solve the problem – should he collaborate with the Allies or not.

Buscaglia died at Naples the day after his accident. He received full military honours in that war-ravaged city.

CHAPTER SIX

WERNER MOLDERS
AND HERMANN GRAF: UNBEATABLE

ON the 11th November, 1940, in a listening post near Calais, a German officer in pilot's uniform, with a thick scarf round his neck, sat motionless at a radio apparatus with the headphones to his ears. His features were drawn and the feverish glitter of his eyes betrayed anxiety.

This officer was Group Commander Werner Mölders, already credited with more than fifty victories. That day a bad attack of flu' had grounded him and he had been forced to hand over the command of the attack to his subordinate and comrade, Lieutenant Claus.

The Battle of Britain, which had been in progress since the beginning of August, was almost lost for the Luftwaffe. No hope now remained of bringing Great Britain to her knees by bombing. The attacking bombers and their fighter escort picked up by radar had to cross murderous anti-aircraft barrages and beat off the attack of the British fighter squadrons which were remarkably well armed and aggressive. The targets were reached less and less often.

Werner Mölders listened over the short wave to the conversation of his pilots on the intercom and realized that they were now engaged with the British defences. Spitfires arrived without cease above the bombers and Stukas, diving on them and starting dog fights with the fighter escorts. Mölders heard exclamations broken by bursts of machine-gun fire.

"Look out. Thirty degrees starboard, same altitude. Three Indians from the ceiling. Get above them."

"*Donnerwetter*, I can't see anything in this rain. Where are they now?"

"Hullo, look out. A fourth on its way down."

His hands clutching the table and bending forward, Mölders was sweating profusely as though he were taking part in the battle. This was, in fact, a more painful ordeal than had he been in the battle, for now the catharsis of action was missing. The noises and shouts of the pilots became more and more confused. One of them – Mölders could not recognize his voice – reported that his machine had been hit and that he was trying to land on the sea in the Thames Estuary. Another shouted: "I'm on fire. I'm baling out."

An orderly came into the room. Mölders removed one of his headphones.

"Lieutenant Eberle has just returned, Herr Kommandant," said the soldier.

Mölders tore off his helmet and ran outside. The pilot had just left his machine and slightly dazed, was staggering towards him in his cumbersome flying suit.

"No ammunition left. It was very tough. I shot down a Spitfire but we suffered losses. Claus was hit several times and had to land in the Thames Estuary."

"So it was him."

Claus, his great pal, who had been with him in so many fights. How many times had he and Mölders helped each other when they had been in a tough spot. He must do everything to try and rescue him. The first thing was to telephone the air-sea rescue.

"You must do the impossible. The impossible, do you understand?"

The airmen on the station no longer recognized their Chief. For the first time they saw him lose his habitual calm. He could not stand still. He was trembling with fever and excitement.

Suddenly he ordered: "Bring me my flying gear and boots, quick. I'll take one of the reserve aircraft. I'm going to find Claus."

"I'm coming with you," said Eberle.

The two aircraft took off in the rain just as the survivors of the operation landed. The mechanics saw them disappear into the grey sky.

Flying almost on top of the waves, Mölders and his companion made for the English coast. They skirted Margate and entered the big, rain-drenched estuary. They were fired on by the coastal batteries but Mölders paid no attention. Nor did he look overhead to see if a Spitfire were about to dive on him. His eyes, famous throughout the Luftwaffe for their eagle quality, were scanning the grey sea in all directions. Not an aircraft on the water. Nothing except dredgers crawling along or an E-boat careering at full speed. Mölders did not shoot at these little vessels for he had only one thought in his head: Claus.

This picture was all that he was to bring back of his comrade. The aircraft was never found. Running short of fuel, he had to return. Mölders' face was ashen when he got out of his aircraft. He kept thinking that had he been in that attack Claus would not have been shot down. But would he not have fallen one day or another. Was that not the fate of a warrior?

A warrior of the air is a very apt description of Werner Mölders. In the opinion of this exceptional fighter – this professional fighter – the fighter pilot had to be primarily a soldier.

"A military education is even more necessary in his case because the fighter pilot is a typically individual combatant," he said. "Each pilot must rigorously observe the discipline of the group and be at the same time capable of leading it."

At a later date when he became Inspector of Fighter Aircraft he put his theories into practice in all squadrons: severe selection, no question of being sent to a fighting unit before being subjected to a thorough military and scientific education and iron discipline. According to the term used by Air Vice Marshal Hébrard, Werner Mölders knew how to reconcile the high tradition of German aviation from the 1914-18 war with the necessities of modern air warfare.

This taste for military tradition was not a matter of chance. Werner Mölders was born in Prussia in the garrison town of Brandenburg in 1913. At the age of four he dragged his mother by the hand to watch the recruits on parade at closer quarters. Boys whom Germany plunged into a long war, took away from school, and sent direct to the battlefield. ...

"I want to be a soldier, *Mutti*," cried the baby.

His mother did not reply. Werner's father, a reserve infantry Lieutenant, had been killed two years before in the Argonne leaving three boys and a girl. Werner was the Benjamin.

His mother brought up her four children without aid. From time to time one of the dead man's brothers invited the little family to stay with him at Trier. Werner was eleven when this uncle said to him: "I'll stand you your first flight. It only costs six marks today."

As he descended from the tourist aircraft, Werner declared: "I'm going to be a pilot officer."

Statistical institutions should be able to furnish details for a study of the number of vocations, casual or accomplished, which resulted from giving children their air baptism. Young Werner originally seems to have been very much thwarted by circumstances. According to the Treaty of Versailles, Germany was only entitled to an army of 100,000 men and allowed no military aviation. But the terms of a Treaty can easily be broken by perseverance and will power.

"I'll begin by being an officer in our small army," said Werner as he left school.

He became this. When he graduated from the Dresden Military Academy as a Second Lieutenant, the German High Command discreetly circulated questionnaires looking for candidates for an eventual air force. Werner Mölders put down his name and was summoned a little later for a medical examination and his endurance tests.

He was placed in front of a blackboard on a swiftly revolving table. When the chair came to a stop, not only was Werner unable to read the letters on the blackboard but he felt giddy and began to vomit.

He was turned down. He was in despair. After a week his will power took the upper hand again. Now that he knew the nature of the physical tests he would train on his own. A few months later he made a second attempt and was accepted.

He was sent to a flying school – civil, of course – where he learned to fly on Junkers 52s.

The re-militarization of the Rhineland constituted the

first serious deliberate violation of the Versailles Treaty. Several civil flying schools were immediately transformed into military stations. Werner Mölders was sent to Schleissheim and given a Stuka. His dream had come true.

The young pilot's superiors had already noticed his qualities of leadership. He left Schleissheim to become instructor to a fighter squadron at Wiesbaden.

At this moment he volunteered for the Condor Legion which fought on Franco's side in the Spanish War. Almost immediately he took command of the third fighter squadron of Galland's wing. Adolf Galland was already a famous German ace. Werner Mölders shot down his first aircraft, a Curtiss, in September, 1938. Two years later he wrote the following lines about this first engagement when he was at Calais. They are particularly interesting because they show Mölders' double vocation – the fighter and the air instructor.

"Today when I think of my first victory I am convinced that it is the most important event in the life of a fighter pilot and I am trying to analyze, as objectively as possible, the impressions one receives. I am even more anxious to do this in my quality of leader in order to help pilots under my command in their first combats.

"I remember that the fact of finding myself for the first time faced with an enemy aircraft gave me a great feeling of joy which overcame my anxiety to know if I were going to apply correctly all that I had learned in the way of aerial combat. The idea that anything might happen to me did not enter my head. Moreover, I do not believe I had time to think. And suddenly I made a mistake by firing far too soon on my first adversary. He got away. Then I drew far too close to the second before firing. He hardly defended himself and went down in flames almost immediately as a result of my fire.

"The first victory may prove decisive in the career of a fighter pilot. This is why I have always helped novices to shoot down their first victim in order to give them confidence. My own personal victories could have been far more numerous had I not invariably followed this policy. But I think that, instead of systematically training a few

111

aces to win the greatest number of victories, it is more useful to form a host of pilots capable of average performances."

When the Spanish War came to a close Mölders was the leading German pilot with fourteen victories. In November, 1938, he was recalled to Germany and in the following year took command of No. 1 Squadron of the "Ace of Spades" Group. This was composed exclusively of pilots who had fought in Spain, and was stationed on the French frontier from the start of hostilities.

I have already mentioned the condition of inequality of material in which the French faced their adversaries from September, 1939, to June, 1940. Despite these conditions the German aces did not pile up very sensational scores during this period, because they were in the majority and fought by rota and because the French pilots proved themselves to be very difficult opponents. Werner Mölders actually shot down seven aircraft during the "phoney" war. He himself was shot down over the forest of Chantilly on 5th June, 1940. Taken prisoner he was liberated by the Franco-German armistice. Promoted to Major he was sent to Calais to take part in what many Germans considered to be the last phase of the war.

The battle for London developed into the Battle of Britain. Mölders' group claimed 500 victories. He himself with a score of sixty aircraft had become Germany's leading ace, Galland being second with forty. But these victories were not "final victory." Great Britain held out; she had survived the critical point and the war continued. Mölders continued to fight. After he had shot down his 115th opponent he was promoted Lieutenant-Colonel and at the same time an order came through from Berlin: "Lieutenant-Colonel Mölders is to report forthwith to General Headquarters and is forbidden to fly."

In most of the belligerent countries the High Commands decided from time to time to stop a great ace in the course of his victories which was also his course towards death. They, of course, may have occasionally thought of the mass of obscure fighting men whom they sent to their deaths, but that was the inevitable price of war whereas the brilliant and mortally dangerous trajectory of fighter pilots impressed these war leaders. Apparently they felt in some way responsible, not only for the fate of a man but for a challenge issued to destiny. Furthermore, they occasionally considered that the amount of experience amassed by one of these exceptional flying men must not be lost but must be communicated. This is the reason for the order: "and is forbidden to fly." None of the leaders ever waited as long as Hitler waited in the case of Mölders. (For another airman, as we shall see later on, Hitler would wait even longer). And yet the Supreme Commander of the Armies of the Third Reich was fully aware of Mölders' value both as an instructor and an organizer. The proof is that shortly after he had been recalled he was promoted Colonel and appointed Inspector of Fighter Aircraft.

Men who are really only alive in the air do not very willingly give up flying. All airmen who have been grounded in this way begin by protesting to their superiors. Now as far as we know, Mölders obeyed without protest although it must have cost him a great deal to have to give up flying. This Prussian knew how to obey as well as how to command and probably thought that he must be the first to set an example of the military spirit. He did his best to carry out his new function.

An Inspector General, whether of aviation or of anything else, usually resides in the capital of his country. He telephones from his office occasionally goes on a tour of inspection. This held good for Mölders' predecessors and it was to hold good for his successors. But Mölders said: "No office – I want a car."

He was given two in which he made his headquarters with telephones and secretaries. The cars either went on trips and Mölders sent his reports to Berlin or else they returned and were parked in the capital for several days. Mölders' interventions not only as inspector of the squadrons but as co-ordinator of the air and land actions reached their maximum efficiency in the spring of 1942 at the time of the big offensive against the Crimea. This offensive was preceded by a formidable aerial preparation. The Inspector's two headquarters cars were driven as near as possible to the front. Every morning Mölders drove his car up to the lines. Leaving his car he walked as far as the trenches and arranged with the Chiefs of various units, the aerial preparations for that day or the following day. Then he returned to his headquarters and telephoned or radioed to the officers commanding the nearby air stations.

He was very busy at this job when he received a telephone call from Goering.

"Udet has just been killed. He is to be given a national funeral. He was the greatest aviator of the last war and you are the greatest of this one. You will be in command of the guard of honour round his tomb. Fly to Berlin at once."

Mölders went immediately to Chaplinka airport near Perekop and boarded a Heinkel 111 with his adjutant, mechanic and wireless operator. The weather was appalling: clouds, rain and a very violent wind. But this was not the first time that Werner Mölders had flown a plane in bad weather. Moreover there was no question of putting off the journey. Udet's guard of honour was waiting for its chief. The Heinkel was airborne and plunged into the storm.

The wind delayed their progress and Mölders decided to land at Breslau to refuel. The visibility was at that moment nil. Mölders lost height on approaching the airfield. The ground was completely invisible. Suddenly one of the engines failed, followed immediately by the second, and a terrible tremor ran through the aircraft. The Heinkel had hit an obstacle – a factory chimney or a telegraph pylon. In a matter of seconds it was a broken carcase lying in the mud. Mölders was killed. In less than twenty-four hours Germany had lost the two best fighter pilots of two generations.

While Werner Mölders was on the Crimean Front he had spotted a Lieutenant Pilot who as yet had few victories to his credit.

"Don't let anything deter you from your path." Mölders said to him as he shook hands. "I've been watching your latest sorties. I predict a great future for you in fighter combat."

The Lieutenant's name was Hermann Graf. Outside his

own country he is not so well-known as the other German aces, for example, Novotny, Pierre Clostermann has devoted several pages in his book to this 22-year-old Lieutenant-Colonel with more than 150 victories to his credit. He was shot down on the 15th March, 1945.

After the war a journalist interviewing Hermann Graf mentioned Novotny and the other great German fighter aces, Mölders, Gollob, Marseille, Hartmann and Rall.

"In your opinion, who was the best?" he was asked.

"We had some very good fighters during the last war," Graf replied. "The best may have been the one whom no one knows anything about. The one who, in his first combat, was abandoned by the luck we all needed so much and who lost his life at the very beginning of his career."

Hermann Graf himself shot down 205 aircraft. This almost incredible figure makes him the record man among fighter pilots of the whole world.

At the beginning of 1940 during the "phoney" war, Hermann Graf was instructor to a squadron stationed in Central Germany. His pupils were only too keen to finish their courses and go to war. He himself certainly wanted to be dispatched to the front since he had chosen a military career.

Like many Germans of his generation he had had difficulties in entering the profession. He had been a factory worker and before being allowed to fly engined aircraft he had been obliged to do many hours gliding; this sport was allowed to conquered Germany and, as is well known, produced a number of excellent pilots.

Hermann Graf therefore had overcome many obstacles before becoming a fighter pilot and doubtless he desired to be sent to the Front. But he nursed a feeling which he kept to himself – he would have preferred to fight against other adversaries than the French. Whenever the name Paris was mentioned in his presence, he looked thoughtful. This name brought back the memory of many tales he had heard at his mother's knee. For her Paris was the most beautiful city in the world. Hermann's mother, who came from an old peasant family living near the Swiss frontier, had gone as a young girl to France and remained there for several years. When she returned to her own country and married there she spoke better French than German. Her husband was an innkeeper and market gardener in the little village of Engen in the Grand Duchy of Baden, twenty miles from Constance. She presented him with several children; Hermann was her youngest son and the one she had loved most tenderly.

Fate was kind to Hermann Graf's secret desire to avoid, if possible, fighting against the French. After a period as instructor, he was sent to Roumania where he remained for a year. Nothing to report from this period. No air battles. At the end of March, 1941, he was posted to a fighter squadron whose task was to support the parachute troops dropped in the conquest of Crete. But this sensational operation, 20th to 31st May, 1941, was then practically over. Hermann Graf with his squadron only flew over the last British warships which were evacuating half the garrison from the south coast.

His real war service began on the 3rd August, 1941, in the Kiev sector of the Russian front. Von Bock was preparing an enormous offensive which was termed "a fury of movement" designed to encircle and destroy twenty-five Soviet divisions. The German aircraft strafed the lines and the enemy rear positions. On that 3rd August, 1941, Hermann Graf met his first enemy, a Russian fighter, and shot him down. On his return he prepared his report with admirable brevity and went to rest. His log book that day only records that he shot down an aircraft. The following is an extract, now published for the first time, from this notebook:

"5th August, 1941. Relative calm last night. A few enemy aircraft fired flares near our camp. Nothing else.

"We are sleeping under canvas in a great tent pitched in the middle of a magnificent field. Straw to sleep on. There are ten of us. We sleep with our clothes on.

"Near my head are two field telephones. I received the orders for tomorrow. Our Captain, who has been recalled to replace the Station Commander, has appointed me Group

Commander. This is the first time I have been given this responsibility.

"Eight fighters will escort an important Stuka formation to attack enemy positions at Kiev. That is the mission. My chief mechanic will warm up the engines at the required time. He has to wake me up a quarter of an hour before take-off.

"It is two o'clock in the morning. I have written down the orders on my writing pad. My Irish setter is asleep on the floor at my side. It is all very romantic. The nervous expenditure of energy during the past few days is having its effect. Some of the pilots talk and rave in their sleep. They re-fight desperate air battles. I try to make out their indistinct words but eventually I fall asleep.

"A rap on my soles woke me up. 'Take-off in a quarter of an hour, *mein Lieutenant*.' We put on our fur boots and lined up beside the aircraft. The engines were already revving.

"I gave the pilots their orders: 'Take off in ten minutes to escort the two groups of Stukas. We fly in sections of two, fifty yards apart. We are to stick to the Stukas and intercept anything that attacks them. The Stukas, heavy and slow with a full bomb load cannot defend themselves.'

"We shook hands irrespective of our rank. We were comrades about to fight together. All watches were synchronized with mine. Another three minutes. We climbed into our aircraft and our mechanics waved.

"The Stukas were already over the airfield gaining height. I raised my hand, full throttle and away.

"Once in the air I checked the formation order and took up my position. We were flying at 9,000 feet.

"Slowly we approached the front line. While we were in Roumania we had been promised that the war in the east would be over in a few weeks. But now we saw the true nature of things. The soil was riddled and pitted with bomb and shell craters. Visions of the 1914-18 war returned to my mind. Were we too condemned to interminable static war with fuel and food becoming ever more hard to obtain?

"The Russian ack-ack went into action. *Zum Teufel!* They fire well. Always just ahead of us which upsets the nerves. Fortunately the Stukas advanced imperturbably without bothering about the enemy fire. I could see them banking slowly away to the left. Their leader must have recognized his targets. We continued to give them cover at close quarters.

"The Commander of the Stukas dived on to the enemy positions followed by his two formations. They tumbled out of the sky one after the other in a vertical dive. A whirlwind of dust arose and the anti-aircraft went on firing.

"Now the Stukas pulled out and were making their way westwards on the home journey. At the start they broke off and avoided the enemy fire as best they could. Then they returned to their close formation.

"I scanned the sky to the east. Suddenly some dots appeared, shining in the sunlight. Russian fighters. For a brief moment I felt excited and then I controlled myself. I gave my orders over the intercom. We manoeuvred to get in the sun and attack.

"The first engagement was very short and the attackers immediately dispersed in all directions. Since some of them seemed about to return we dived on them. A few seconds fighting and they turned back eastwards. We were unable to shoot any down but the Stukas were now safely over our lines. Our mission was completed.

"A few minutes later we landed. The Stuka pilots shook our hands and their Commanding Officer thanked us. We returned to our own camp. A report and a criticism of the operation. ... Everyone, irrespective of rank, was allowed to give his opinion. Even a private soldier can have an inspired or interesting idea."

30th April, 1942. The war in the east continued. The Russians delivered their first counter offensive during the winter. At first a few sporadic thrusts and harassing actions, more in the nature of guerilla warfare than a real battle, followed by organized attacks. The German troops, shivering in their inadequate clothing, forced to defend their lines of communication and supply over enormous distances, yielded ground in front of Moscow, Tula, Kursk, all along the front, about a tenth of the territory conquered. "An elastic defence," announced the Berlin communiques. It is true that the German military potential had not diminished. On the contrary, it had increased since the beginning of the war. The whole world was waiting for the new German offensive.

On a German airfield in the Crimea while it was still dark, a score of pilots in their flying suits slowly approached their aircraft, casting a glance at their watches. The engines had been warmed up and then stopped. The cool night was completely silent.

Suddenly, like a signal, came a dull isolated thud. The pilots stopped. An enormous rumble made itself heard, growing louder and uninterrupted. The preparation for the great offensive against Kerch had just begun.

The Crimean campaign, however, was continued throughout the winter and the beginning of spring. The German High Command envisaged the conquest of Kerch as the prelude to a vast strategic target, Sevastopol, the key to the Black Sea. For several days numerous units of the Luftwaffe had been assembling in the peninsula. The bombers attacked enemy positions night and day.

The fighter pilots who were about to take off at dawn on the 30th April had received orders to prevent the Russian aviation from taking the air and participating in the battle. The officer commanding one of these groups was the Lieutenant for whom Werner Mölders predicted a brilliant future when he had shaken hands with him a few weeks before. He was Hermann Graf.

"This was the finest moment in my career as a pilot," Graf maintained after the war. "The greatest of them all had spoken to me and had instilled me with self-confidence." An extremely effective inoculation, to judge by Hermann Graf's score on the eve of the Kerch battle: sixty-nine confirmed victories. The Inspector of Fighter Aircraft had not been mistaken. He had indicated the pilot who was to have the most fantastic career ever known.

Hermann Graf was now flying with his unit. He arrived

over the first enemy airfield. Three Russian fighters were just taking off. Graf gave his orders over the intercom. "I'll look after them. You cruise over the airfield and attack everything that leaves the ground."

He flew past the three Russians, did a loop and dived on them *on his back*. "In this way the dive brought me to within a few feet of the ground at over 400 m.p.h. My hedge-hopping speed protected me from the Russian anti-aircraft which kept blazing away at me." Graf came to the first Russian, opened fire at point-blank range, and disengaged. The burning Soviet aircraft ran into his nearest comrade and both of them crashed. "Seventieth and seventy-first victory – I was very lucky."

At that moment a Russian squadron from another aerodrome appeared out of the sky. "They took us completely by surprise and there was a dog fight. I had great difficulty in carrying out a classic attack. But we soon recovered and two of my pilots accounted for one of the enemy while I managed to bring down my seventy-second. We returned to our airfield."

At midday Graf took off again with his unit and once more made contact with the enemy. He shot down four aircraft. "The day the big offensive opened was my record day with seven victories."

He did not give any other details and in future he gave less and less about these victorious combats which he carried out at full speed very close to the ground whenever he could, for this proximity often disturbed or paralysed his opponent while he could manoeuvre with the greatest skill in the most difficult conditions. During this Crimean battle he shot down thirty of the enemy in three weeks. "Luck was with me," he wrote in his diary. Luck, maybe, but not only that.

His skill and the luck which favoured him did not turn him into a "death or glory boy" or make him forget the safety of his pilots – as far as a group commander can bother about such things during an offensive. Thus one day during this same Crimean battle he received his order to attack a Russian aerodrome near Sevastopol. His first reaction on reading the order attentively was to raise objections at wing headquarters and to advise against the operation. It was too dangerous. The results hoped for would not be worth the risks involved. Coming from a pilot like Hermann Graf these objections must have been examined seriously. The reply came back, however: "Carry out orders received."

Here is an account of this operation.

"It was still dark when we left our tents. Fate decided once more against me and my group. We shook hands thinking that none of us would return. We knew the merits of the Russian anti-aircraft and considered it to be the best in the world. It maintained the great traditions of the Russian artillery, nothing complicated but admirable aiming. This was one of the disagreeable surprises the Russian war had reserved for us.

"The sun rose as we crossed the Black Sea. We could see the Turkish coast. Soon we flew over the Russian lines at 12,000 feet and then the coast. Now we were a long way from the shore. Our plan of attack had been particularly well thought out in order to reduce our losses to a minimum. Last night I myself made a reconnaissance flight of today's route (at high altitude).

"We banked and set our course northwards in the direction of the coast. For a few moments we flew in close formation above the sea with the sun behind us protected by a light early morning mist.

"I glanced at the sun. Should I ever see it again? I also thought of my mother. I was sure that she would not long survive my death.

"We flew at just over 300 m.p.h. The automatic weapons were ready for firing. Right fore-finger on the trigger, my thumb on the button on top of the joystick, ready to fire my cannon. The little finger pressed the intercom apparatus. Two fingers and the palm of my hand therefore left to fly the aircraft.

"There was the rock I had spotted yesterday. We climbed rapidly to cross the cliffs but then immediately went down to ground level over enemy territory. My nerves were at breaking point. Forcing myself to keep a calm voice I shouted over the intercom: 'Good luck.'

"Just ahead of me on the horizon I could see the hangars. Suddenly all my depression disappeared. I had no thoughts except for the attack.

"We arrived over our target exactly on schedule. I saw the Russian soldiers running in all directions as the ack-ack began to fire. We flew at ground level among the tracer bullets.

"One of my experiences from a few weeks earlier suddenly crossed my mind. It was a dive attack on an airfield at Dnepropetrovsk. The aircraft of two of my comrades flying just ahead of me exploded in the air. I flew through the incandescent debris of two aircraft – a horrible sight. Would this be my fate? I saw five Russian machines on the ground and we fired into them with all our weapons. An ack-ack battery at the edge of the airfield picked us up. In a couple of seconds we silenced it. I held my breath. But there was no time to think. We were experiencing the most brutal form of this pitiless war.

"I recovered my breath. Nothing had happened to me. Now we were in the no man's land between the airfield and the enemy lines. I glanced at my thermostat to see if a burst had hit my radiators and I was sure that my comrades were doing the same. But all was well. I zoomed, followed by the others and we were already at 12,000 feet. Safe, and incredible as it may seem, no-one missing.

"We flew over our own lines at 15,000 feet. We met our reconnaissance aircraft which, according to plan, had been observing the results of our attack.

"A few hours later we examined the aerial photos taken by this observer. Several of the enemy aircraft were in flames; the attack had not been in vain. But we were all rather silent and our nerves had been badly shaken by this operation."

On the 28th July, 1942, von Bock's tanks crossed the Don by surprise between Nikolayevsk and Tsymlyanskaya and began to climb up the left bank of the river. They were halted in front of Tsymlyanskaya by the Russians who, for the first time, used their special anti-tank guns. These were fired at close range by crews of two men.

"Well," said von Bock. "We must cross the Don in front of Stalingrad and by-pass the town from the north and the south."

The greatest battle in history had begun.

Its first phase was played out in the dusty burning desert of the summer steppe. Several times a day Stuka formations escorted by fighters attacked the city and the enemy positions. The German airfields were of a temporary nature without the least comfort – a few huts, tents and scores of aircraft standing wing tip to wing tip. The men had the impression of living in a strange universe, remote from this earth. The letters they received from home, from a Germany already suffering the effects of war really seemed to arrive from another world; there was mention of women and children, of shops and railways. They themselves knew only war in all its nudity.

Hermann Graf was in this battle at the head of his group. He had been sent to this new sector in the Crimea. Life under canvas continued with orders given over the telephone, the study of a map folded on one's knees by torchlight. Take-offs before dawn. Aerial photos allowed them to recognize every enemy position and every house in Stalingrad.

Escorting Stukas, interception of Russian formations, attacks on airfields – these were the missions. At one time Hermann Graf was called "The King of the Hedge-hopping Attack" but now they merely said "Hermann Graf." That was enough. It was generally admitted that no one could be compared with him in audacity, skill and efficiency. Two, three, four, five times a day he was airborne with his group, adding to his innumerable victories. His pilots heard his calm, clear voice in their headphones, organizing the attack with incredible self-confidence as though this leader had been able to foresee each of his adversaries' movements.

He himself flew at the head of his formation and every enemy aircraft on which he dived could *a priori* be considered as shot down. On his return he would say: "Yes, I was lucky." And he would immediately begin to criticise the operation, asking the opinion of the other pilots. In his diary after August, 1942, he did not note down anything except certain aspects of the life of the pilots and a few reflections about the war. No details of his individual battles. For an artiste who has completely mastered his technique, detail does not matter; it is taken for granted.

The fantastic career of Hermann Graf had been followed by the German High Command in Berlin. Several times already at the 150th and again at the 160th and 180th victories, Goering had asked Hitler: "Isn't it time to stop him?"

Hitler had not replied. At Graf's 200th victory Goering took it upon himself to send the telegram: "You are forbidden to fly." Before he received the message Graf had shot down another two. 202 victories!

Now came a long interval. Retired from the Front and from the sky, busy with staff work, Hermann Graf, who had officially become the "hero of Stalingrad", only participated in the offensive phase of that gigantic battle (28th July, 1942, to 2nd February, 1943, with millions of men engaged).

He did not take part in the halt of the advance, in the siege which was a mortal stagnation. From the air he did not see the agony of the sick army which marked the beginning of the German defeat. In the midst of this tragic defeat he was a survivor of the era of offensives, a conqueror, immobilized and turned into a monument by a ban on his flying.

The ban on the Commodore of the Graf Squadron was maintained while his unit continued to fight above the German armies retreating from Russia, Poland and Silesia. He followed from afar the exploits of his former subordinates, counting their victories which became more useless week by week. . . .

Then came the final disaster. During the night of the 23rd/24th March, 1945, Montgomery's troops crossed the Rhine. Two days later Eisenhower launched eight armies against the heart of Germany, towards which 1,500 heavy bombers constantly renewed and escorted by as many fighters cleaved a path, pulverizing the cities. At this juncture the rumour ran round among the remnants of the fighter squadron still trying to defend the German sky in the west: "Hermann Graf is with us. He's back in action."

It was true. The grounded Commodore, the man with 202 victories to his credit, could no longer bear to watch the collapse of his country. "Forbidden to fly." What did these words now mean? Who was going to check if such an order had been transgressed in this chaos, when whole divisions found themselves cut off from H.Q. and were fighting on their own initiative or giving up? Hermann Graf disobeyed the order and managed to return to the west front, to one of those strafed airfields with burning hangars and pitted with bomb craters from which the pilots took off as though in a dream for their last combats.

On the 29th March, 1945, in a gale of wind, Graf took off with three of his squadron – four aircraft! – to attack an American squadron. Hardly were the Messerschmitts airborne than they were detected by the infallible radar and attacked. Hermann Graf's three comrades, surrounded by a horde of American fighters, succumbed. He himself, after shooting down one, took a second. His 204th victory. Now he was alone in the air, surrounded by the enemy swarm. Black smoke was already belching from one of his engines. What young pilot from Wisconsin or Oklahoma was going to finish off this German Luftwaffe ace of aces – the world champion fighter pilot?

Alone in his cockpit, Hermann Graf closed his eyes for a second, "To think," as he said. And he made up his mind. *If I've got to die it might as well be as a conqueror.* In a last manoeuvre he managed to right his machine which was losing height, and waded in at full throttle at the nearest of the American aircraft. There was a tremendous shock. The two aircraft broke up in the air simultaneously and their wings drifted slowly down to earth.

From the fuselage of the aircraft with black crosses, a kind of bundle detached itself. Hermann Graf had managed to bale out. Probably in bad conditions, for the bundle increased in speed as it neared the ground. The American formation flew off on its way.

The parachute opened with a report so near the ground that normally the German airman should have been killed. On impact, he did not hit the ground but the water of a pond. The surface was agitated and whipped up by a strong wind. Carried away, with his parachute forming a sail, Hermann Graf felt himself being blown towards the shore. Hardly had he touched land than he clung on to some reeds and fainted.

When he recovered consciousness he saw two men running towards him. He did not know whether they were civilians or soldiers. In his befuddled state he could not be certain of anything. Two of the enemy, he thought, and instinctively felt for his revolver to wage what he considered to be "his last fight." Then he remembered immediately: *Verflucht! I left it in the Mess when the alert went.* It was a lucky omission, for the two men who arrived were not the enemy but two German peasants who took the Commodore to the nearest hospital.

Nevertheless the High Command of the Luftwaffe had learned of Hermann Graf's flight and that he had been brought down in aerial combat. The German radio broadcast appeals to know whether he or his body had been discovered. The Allied radio heard these broadcasts and in the American squadrons the pilots paid tribute to an esteemed enemy who had fallen in loyal combat: a remarkable state of affairs in the middle of a war of attrition.

No. 52 Squadron of the Luftwaffe, the Hermann Graf squadron, mourned its chief. It received inaccurate and conflicting reports. The Commodore was alive; he had died from wounds; or his fate was unknown. Nothing could be known for certain in Germany during the collapse, now that all communications had been cut. For his former comrades in arms an aura of mystery surrounded the figure of Hermann Graf, creating of him a kind of glorious myth which would survive the defeat.

For now it really was the end. Unconditional surrender. No. 52 Squadron had fought its last battles in Bohemia over Marshal Schörner's Panzer divisions. Came the 8th May, 1945. The previous day at 02.41 hours, in the precincts of Rheims Technical College, the emissaries of Grand

Admiral Doenitz, Major-General Gustav Jodl and General Admiral von Friedeburg had signed the unconditional surrender of all the German military forces.

Article 2 of the preliminary act of capitulation read as follows: "The German High Command will immediately give orders to all the military, naval and air authorities to cease active operations at 23.01 hours Central European Time on the 8th May and to remain in the positions occupied at that hour. No ship, vessel or aircraft must be scuttled and no damage whatsoever is to be inflicted on their hulls, their machines or their equipment."

For the pilots of No. 52 Squadron who were encircled in a pocket near Brünn this meant waiting, not touching their aircraft, until the Russians arrived and took them prisoner. These men who had so often been victorious in the sky were stupefied and bewildered.

That morning an officer in the greatest agitation came into the Mess and said. "The Commodore is alive. He has returned to us. I've just seen him in the C.O.'s tent." Hardly had he finished speaking than Hermann Graf entered the Mess. Some of those present were so amazed that they forgot to stand up. Commodore Hermann Graf – was it possible? The youngest pilots of the squadron had never seen him. They stared at him as though they had seen a ghost. He spoke to them quietly.

"I have managed to get back. The order for capitulation will not come into force until tonight at 23.01 hours. I have decided that we will not surrender with our aircraft. None of our enemies shall touch the joy stick of our aircraft upon which our life has depended for so many years. I am giving the order to destroy all the aircraft remaining to us."

A little later Hermann Graf addressed the whole personnel of the squadron.

"Your officers, at my suggestion, have decided to remain with you. As brothers in arms we have shared our joys, cares and sorrows. We shall submit together to our uncertain fate which may mean to perish together or to live together. We are going to burn our aircraft so that they do not fall into the hands of the enemy. The war is over and lost but we will not surrender to the Russians; we will surrender to the Americans. We will go together to their lines, fighting our way through if necessary. From this moment the Graf Squadron will become the Graf Storm Regiment."

The men cheered their Commandant. The aircraft bearing the squadron emblem, the winged sword on a scarlet and gold background, were sprinkled with petrol and burnt. When all of them had been transformed into flaming torches the Graf Storm Regiment fell in and began its march towards the west.

The decision to retire on the whole eastern front to the western front line as swiftly as possible had been taken on the 7th May by the Schörner Air Corps Staff. Several columns advanced west through Czechoslovakia, sometimes running into Russian armour. Some of them laid down their arms in accordance with the armistice terms, but the Russians let some of them continue on their way. Sometimes the unarmed columns were exterminated by groups of Czech partisans in civilian clothes. Everywhere towns in ruins were burning, hosts of people were fleeing along the roads in carts and on foot – a desperate stream making its way to the west. The Graf Storm Regiment fought its way through. There were occasional skirmishes with Russians intoxicated by their victory but more often occupied in taking their revenge on the country of their terrible war years than determined to bar the way to this resolute troop which would, in any case, be captured.

The Storm regiment arrived almost in complete strength and in good order at the American lines. Hermann Graf declared to the first American officer he met that he had come to surrender his former squadron as an independent unit.

The name of Hermann Graf was not unknown to the Allied airmen. The conquerors ran up to see with their own eyes this famous fighter, the man with 205 victories whom they had believed to be dead. The Commodore, his officers and men, after being taken prisoner, were well treated and shown some consideration.

"Ten days relaxation with the Americans," were the

words used by Hermann Graf. But on the eleventh day, the officer who had accepted his surrender came to him and said: "The terms of the Armistice are imperative. Your unit was in the Russian Zone at the moment Germany capitulated and we have to deliver you to the Russians. I'm sorry. Our armoured cars will escort you to their lines." The men of the Graf Storm Regiment fell in for the last time. Their C.O. reviewed them and then took up his position at their head. The unit set out for the east between two lines of American tanks.

Hermann Graf is still alive. He remained four and a half years as a prisoner in Russia. Sometimes in his hut at night he took off the heel of one of his shoes and brought from it a piece of paper which he unfolded and re-read by the light of a candle. This paper contained a copy of the report which he had written to the last Supreme Commander of the Luftwaffe on the day of the capitulation after he had crossed Germany in ruins and flames to rejoin his unit. The Commodore had preserved this relic in the face of all searchings. It was the only private paper remaining to him which still proved to the captive lost in this immense flock that he really was Hermann Graf.

He was liberated after four and a half years spent behind Russian barbed wire. Today he lives with his brother, where he has changed two rooms into a modest air museum filled with various souvenirs. Occasionally some of his former comrades pay him a visit. What should these men speak of except the years which were the most intense of their lives? After they have left and he remains alone with his memories and with his dream, it is the dream of all those who have known the intoxication of being airborne – to fly another day.

CHAPTER SEVEN

BONG AND McGUIRE:
A MATCH TO THE FINISH

ON the 7th July, 1942, at ten o'clock in the morning General Kenney, Officer Commanding the Fourth American Air Force, found a report on the table of his office in San Francisco. It intimated that a young subaltern pilot named Richard Bong had found it amusing to loop the loop round the central span of the bridge over the Golden Gate. Later he had flown along several streets of the city and the neighbourhood below roof-top height. As a result of this the Chief of Police had received a host of letters of protest which he had forwarded to Washington. An investigating officer had been appointed. The file had returned the night before to General Kenney with copies of the letters of protest. One of them came from a woman in Oakland who said she had no need of airmen to blow away her washing hanging out on the line. The enquiring officer spoke of the security of the civilian population and eventually called for a court martial for the delinquent.

A secretary looked through the door.

"Sir, the pilot you sent for is here in the waiting room. The acrobat."

"Show him in," said the General.

He stared at the door with marked ferocity. This hothead was going to find out who he was talking to, and no mistake.

The "hothead" came in and stood to attention. The General had to make a great effort not to betray his surprise. A cherub stood in front of him, a fair-haired pale-pink adolescent who seemed to be hardly eighteen. A round infantile face with huge innocent blue eyes in which terror could be read. ... The General looked away and stood up. He cleared his throat and began to shout: "Well, have you gone completely nuts? I tell you straight away that the Fourth Air Force is not a troop of irresponsible jockeys. Do you see that pile of papers? That's your file. All that's on your account. Are you feeling proud of yourself? Because of you. I've got the Governor, the Mayor and the Chief of Police on my tail. Do you think I find that funny?"

The cherub did not reply. His pink face had turned a trifle pale. The General looked down at the papers once more, stacked them together, grumbling, and shrugged his shoulders. When he looked up he thought that the acrobat, still standing there to attention, was on the point of being sick.

"Do you know that you risk being chucked out of the service?"

A faint voice replied: "Yes, sir, so I've been told."

"Stand easy!" said the General.

He looked through his papers again. "Tell me," he said suddenly, "weren't you at all hampered by air currents, flying along the streets on a level with the second storey?"

"Maybe a bit, sir, but I was in perfect control of the machine. The aileron control is perfect on the P.48."

The reply came out instantaneously and colour had returned to the boy's cheeks. Then he fell silent again and his expression was once more one of fright. The General closed his file.

"This is all very serious," he said. "I'll have you know that had you never felt any urge to do what you've done I should consider you unworthy of serving in the Fourth Air Force. But you're not to repeat this exploit. Get that clear. If ever I hear any more of you in a story of this nature it will be a court martial, and I'll have you kicked out."

The General picked up the report and began to tear it up, flinging the pieces in the waste-paper basket. He looked at the pilot out of the corner of his eye. His blue eyes seemed to grow darker and his face to flush. The General handed him a letter.

"On Monday morning you will go to this address; it's the day the woman does her washing. You will help her hang it out to dry. Try and make yourself really useful for once. If you drop any of it you will wash it again yourself. I want this woman to realize that aviators are good for something else besides annoying people. Now, Bong, run along before I get really steamed up and change my mind. That's all!"

"Yes, sir."

A second later he had disappeared. The General began to roar with laughter.

In September, 1942, two cargo ships from the United States carrying fifty twin-engine fighter bombers, Lightning P.38s, sailed into Brisbane Harbour. The pilots who had come by air were already on the spot. They immediately began to undergo intensive training for the battle against the Japanese. Among them was the pilot, Richard Bong, who in the meantime had been promoted Lieutenant.

He was in action for the first time on the 27th September, 1942, while his unit was based at Laloki in New Guinea. The engagement in which twelve P.38s were in a fight with twenty-five Japanese bombers and fighters took place over Dobodura, the occupied Japanese base. The P.38s shot down fifteen enemy aircraft, Richard Bong claiming two of them.

General Kenney flew from Brisbane to Laloki to congratulate the pilots. He asked to see Bong's report. In it there was only mention of the hour of take-off, the time of arrival over Dobodura, the shooting down of the two Japanese aircraft and the time of his landing. Nothing else.

"Watch that boy," said General Kenney to his colleague, General Whitehead. "He will be the American ace of this war, unless I'm very much mistaken."

Richard Bong continued to fly and to fight in his P.38 along the north coast of New Guinea where the American troops were making slow progress, pushing back the Japanese. The missions were very varied and often difficult because of the climate and the nature of the country – a jungle, surrounded by high mountains over which the enemy suddenly appeared. The Japanese were very aggressive. The American fighters took off quickly to meet their formations and escorted the bombers to attack the Japanese bases. Certain of these attacks, like those which took place above Rabaul, in the Solomon Islands, were delivered at very low altitudes on the vessels moored in the harbours and in the roadsteads. The airmen saw ships catch fire and sink, petrol tanks explode, while the Japanese ack-ack fired furiously and their speedy Zeros buzzed round them like swarms of wasps. The Zeros were extremely handy but fragile. Their pilots showed indisputable audacity. The Americans shot down a great many of them and their own losses were slightly less.

By the beginning of January, 1944, Lieutenant Richard Bong had shot down nineteen Japanese aircraft of different types. He was one of the "Big Three" of the South-West Pacific in company with Colonel Neel Kearby (nineteen victories) and Lieutenant-Colonel Tommy Lynch (sixteen victories). Another pilot who had baled out and been fished out of the sea during one of the big bombing attacks on Rabaul had a score of eleven, eight less than Bong. He was a small, black-moustached captain named Tommy McGuire.

In February, 1944, when Bong returned from leave, his unit was still in New Guinea at Nadzab, near Lae. His group commandant sent for him.

"Intelligence has decoded an enemy message stating that a Japanese aircraft will arrive this evening at 18.00 hours precisely at Wewack, with a V.I.P. on board. As you can see on the map, Wewack is 450 miles up the coast from here. You will take off immediately with Lieutenant Tommy Lynch and try to intercept this aircraft."

450 miles was a long way. Tommy Lynch and Richard Bong set out at full throttle. They arrived at Wewack at 17.58 hours. The Japanese transport plane had just landed and was taxiing along the runway. Tommy Lynch was the first to attack. Once in his dive he noticed that he had forgotten to set his aiming gear. His attack was a failure. "Your turn, Bong!" he cried over the intercom. Bong dived and fired a single burst. The Japanese aircraft exploded. No one had time to get out of it. About a hundred Japanese who had been walking across the runway, presumably to greet the visitors, were flung to the ground by the explosion or remained frozen to the spot. Lynch and

Bong took advantage of this to let them have a few bursts and then flew off.

On their return General Kenney summoned them to his office.

"We heard a feverish exchange of radio messages between Tokyo and Wewack immediately after your attack," he said. "The aircraft contained two Generals and a whole staff. Now make your report." Lynch told the story and Bong nodded his head.

"If the aircraft was on the ground when it blew up it can't count on your score," the General said to Bong.

"I'm well aware of that, sir."

"But are you absolutely certain that it was on the ground," the General went on. "It may have bounced a little after landing. If it was a hand's-breadth above the runway you can count it."

Lynch smiled and Bong listened with a serious face.

"No, sir," he said, without the slightest trace of disappointment. "It was on the ground. In fact it had completely stopped."

On the 22nd April, 1944, during the last bombing of Hollandia in New Guinea, Richard Bong shot down his 27th aircraft, thus beating the record of Eddie Rickenbacker – the leading American Ace of World War I.

"I don't want this fine pitcher to go too often to the well," said General Kenney to his chief of staff. "This is a good opportunity to send him for a rest to the States."

He summoned Bong.

"Bong, I've decided to promote you to major. You will go on leave to Wisconsin and let your fiancee admire your new uniform. I think you will be acclaimed wherever you go as one of the American aces of this war, which is only your due. Then what would you say to a little spell at a firing school? I think you yourself mentioned this idea to me."

"Yes, sir, I should like to take a firing course," said Bong. "Thank you very much, sir."

Strange though it may seem, Bong was not a very good shot. He shot down the Japanese aircraft because he fired at almost point-blank range. His skill in aerobatics allowed him to do this, but from a distance he was definitely a bad shot.

"Well, that's okay," said the General. "Have you any other request?"

"I should like to say a word about that aircraft I shot down on April 12 above Hollandia, sir. It was not counted in my score because no one except me saw it fall."

"Well, what of it?"

"I have marked on a photo the exact place where it fell in the water just near the coast. It was a single-seater of the type we call an Oscar. I hit the left wing and the pilot as well as the engine, but it did not catch fire. I thought we might be able to salvage it now that Hollandia is in our hands."

"Very well, Bong, I'll see to it."

A little later, the General sent a diver down at the precise point indicated by Bong. The aircraft was there. It was an Oscar with eleven bullets in the left wing; the pilot had been shot in the head and neck and two cylinders of the engine had been destroyed. It bore no traces of fire. It was added to Bong's score: 28 victories.

After finishing his firing course Richard Bong returned to the South-West Pacific. General Kenney brought him once more to his headquarters, which were now in Hollandia.

"Well, how did things go at home?" asked the General.

"Very well, sir. Thank you very much for letting me take that course. I'm terrified to think of the amount of ammunition I must have wasted to shoot down 28 enemy aircraft. I think I shall be more economical in future. If you agree, I should like to see how I've got on by taking my place straight away in a fighter squadron."

"This is what you are going to do," said the General. "You will go on tour to the different fighter bases in the neighbourhood and pass on to the pilots the instruction you have just received. If you can only teach about a hundred of them to shoot down a Japanese aircraft with a single burst you will do a better job than by fighting yourself. I'm making you an instructor."

Bong seemed only half-satisfied.

"In the meantime I authorize you to fly with your pupils if they are recommended to fly on a mission," continued the General. "But don't try to hog the fight for yourself. Watch the results obtained by your pupils and see if they have learned from your lessons. Only fight if you are attacked. Do you understand?"

"Yes, sir."

On the following day General Kenney received a visit from Captain Tommy McGuire, the small black-moustached pilot who had been shot down and fished out of the sea during the big attack on Rabaul.

"Sir," said McGuire. "I've come to ask you to lift the flying ban which has been imposed on me by the doctors."

"If they've forbidden you to fly, they must have some reason. You don't look too good to me."

"I've had an attack of malaria, sir, but I'm all right now. That's why I'd like to start flying again at once. When I arrived at this theatre of war in the spring of 1943, Richard Bong had eight victories and naturally I had none. I began to bring down the Japs but each time I brought down one or two, Bong did the same. When he had a score of nineteen I had eleven – always eight behind, and this has gone on. When he was sent back to the States he stood at 28 and I was 20. This is my chance, I said to myself, it will be hell if during his trip down there I don't catch him up. At that moment I fell sick. I only got out of hospital yesterday and have been grounded for ten days. I'm still eight behind and in ten days time God knows how many Japs Bong will have brought down."

"Don't worry yourself," said the General. "I've just made Bong an instructor. He's agreed not to fight except in cases of legitimate self-defence. He can't add to his score for the moment. You've plenty of time. Take your ten days' rest and everything will be okay."

On the 10th October, General Kenney sent the following telegram to General Arnold, commanding the American Aviation: "In the course of the bombing of Balikpapan today, Major Richard Bong accompanied the fighter aircraft with orders to observe the results of the fighting instruction he has given the young pilots since his return from the United States. He found himself in a position of self-defence and shot down two Japanese aircraft. Although it is regrettable, this brings his official score to 30 enemy aircraft shot down in aerial combat. I have requested Bong to continue to be more prudent." General Arnold replied: "Congratulations to Major Bong for his mastery in the important art of self-defence. I am sure that your recommendation will have the desired effect." These two telegrams are quoted textually. They were posted on the notice-board and McGuire got to learn of them. Three days later he received permission to fly. He took part in a mission and shot down two Japanese, thus bringing his score to 22. Still eight behind Bong.

On the 25th October, 1944, General Kenney arrived in an aircraft at Tacloban in the Island of Leyte in the Phillipines, where he had just installed his new head-quarters. General McArthur was with him. The sapper specialists immediately began to rebuild the air base which they had captured from the Japanese. Their work was frequently interrupted by enemy bombing attacks. On the 27th, however, General Kenney could wire to General Whitehead in New Guinea: "Quarters ready for 34 P.38s."

The aircraft arrived at midday. Kenney and McArthur broke off their lunch to welcome the pilots.

The last to get out of his plane was Major Richard Bong. Kenney called to him and McArthur shook his hand.

"Who told you to come here?" asked Kenney.

"I have permission from General Wurtshith and General Whitehead," Bong replied gently.

"Did they tell you you could fight?"

"No, sir, but can I?"

Kenney shrugged his shoulders and the other officers laughed.

"We are in such a pickle here that anyone capable of flying a P.38 should be authorized to fight. The answer's 'yes'."

"Good, sir."

At 17.00 hours five Japanese aircraft were sighted. Five P.38s took off to intercept them, including Richard Bong who shot down a Japanese. On the following day, the 28th, he took off on a mission to look for places suitable for building airfields in the neighbourhood. In the course of this mission he met two Japanese aircraft which he shot down in two bursts.

On the 30th October, McGuire landed at Tacloban with his unit. In the course of the trip the P.38s had met an enemy patrol and shot down six Japanese – one more for McGuire.

"My score is now twenty-three," he said. "How many has Bong got?"

"Thirty-three," was the answer.

He rectified this on the following day by shooting down two more. Bong, 33; McGuire, 25; eight behind.

The whole of the American Air Force in the South-West Pacific began to enthuse about this extraordinary match. Richard Bong never referred to it and did not even seem to know that it was going on. McGuire, the challenger, spoke about it freely.

The fact that the Japanese pilots were now less experienced than those during the initial stages of the war allowed the two aces to increase their respective scores fairly quickly. 34 to 26; 36 to 28, 38 to 30. However, the game was still dangerous enough. Not only did the P.38s attack formations of Zeros and Japanese bombers but they took part in low altitude attacks on convoys against artillery and troop positions, during which they were sometimes exposed to very heavy ack-ack fire. The Japanese were now using suicide aircraft, Kamikazes, flown by mediocre pilots who, however, displayed a complete indifference to death.

The American Air Force and Navy began to suffer losses. ...

On the 12th December, 1944, six P.38s were lined up in a semi-circle on the airfield of Tacloban. Before a guard of honour composed of twelve pilots, each of whom had a dozen victories to his credit, stood Major Richard Bong looking almost as self-conscious as on the day at San Francisco when General Kenney had sent for him to reprimand him. He was to receive the Congressional Medal of Honour from the hands of General McArthur.

Punctual to the minute, McArthur appeared on the airfield, advanced towards Bong, and stopped a few paces away from him. Bong saluted; McArthur returned the salute and put both hands on the pilot's shoulders. General McArthur was marvellously at ease in all solemn circumstances required of him. He raised his voice.

"Of all the military virtues, the one that inspires the greatest admiration is courage. The United States Congress has reserved for itself the honour of decorating those who, above all, appear as brave men among the brave. It is in this high and noble category, Major Bong, that you are now placed as I pin on your breast the Medal of Honour. Wear it as the symbol of the invincible courage that you have shown in combat. My dear boy, may a merciful God continue to protect you. Such is the prayer of your Commanding Officer."

Two thousand spectators – airmen, officers and soldiers of all services, war correspondents and Phillipinos – were present at the ceremony. Richard Bong, congratulated and harried on all sides, managed to slip away from this crowd and to take refuge with his Group Commander.

"Sir, I forgot to have lunch this morning," he said. "Have you got anything for me?"

Two days later in the late afternoon, General Kenney learned that Bong and McGuire had each shot down one more aircraft. The novelty of this news consisted in the fact that two pilots had fought together although belonging to two different squadrons. Anxious to learn more details the General took his jeep and made for McGuire's hut. He entered without knocking and found the two men taking a shower.

"I must apologize," said the General. "I'll sit down while you get dressed, but tell me briefly about this morning."

As usual it was McGuire who told the story.

"Well, it was like this, sir, the pilots of Bong's squadron think he is a jinx to them. As soon as they meet some

Japanese, Bong shoots down one or two. The others take a powder and there's nothing left for the boys. So he came this morning and asked me if he could fly with my squadron. After some hesitation I said 'yes'. I had to leave on a recce of the local Japanese airfield and I suggested that Bong should accompany me. We each took off with a 'winger'.

"At first we found nothing and we were on the point of returning when I saw a group of Oscars. I thought that Bong had not spotted them. I called to my 'winger' over the intercom to follow me, or rather I whispered it so that Bong should not hear. I dived on the Japs and shot one down with a single burst. I turned back with the intention of diving on the second but that devil of a Bong was already on him. I saw the Jap explode and Bong returned to my side, dipping his wings. Result – I'm still eight behind him. At the end of the war it won't be difficult to find a nickname for me: 'Eight Behind'."

Three days later McGuire agreed once more that Bong should accompany him on a fighter party of the same type. Each of them shot down a Jap. Bong 40; McGuire 32. General Kenney sent for Richard Bong.

"My boy," he said to him. "I want to keep you alive. You've more than done your duty. From now onwards and until further orders, no more fighting! That's an order. You're going to become a firing instructor again and this time in the States. I'm sending you back home as soon as I have a place available for you on board a transport plane. In the meanwhile you will be an instructor here."

The General went on for a moment to say that the first duty of every fighting man was to submit to discipline and that the responsible chiefs were the best judges as to the best use to which their pilots could be put.

"So," thumping Bong on the shoulders, he said: "Don't get depressed. After a spell in the States we'll see if there's any hope of letting you fight once more."

"Yes, sir."

Richard Bong obviously could only submit. This acceptance, however, must have cost him a great deal, for although he was never talkative and always ill at ease at moments when he was feted and honoured there is every good reason to think that, in his heart, like so many other champions, he attached a very great value to his score.

McGuire's moment had arrived. On Christmas Day, 1944, while escorting bombers over Mabacacat, he shot down two Japanese. The following day his squadron repulsed an enemy raid on Clarkfield Airfield. He shot down four Japanese that day, bringing his total up to 38. 'Eight behind' now became two behind, and there was no chance of Richard Bong increasing his score. General Kenney sent for McGuire. "You don't look at all well, lad. Unless you take care of yourself you will have another bout of malaria. I'm going to ground you for a few days."

"But you can't do that to me, sir," exclaimed the pilot. He went on quickly, "I'm sorry, sir, but think: I'm only two victories short of Bong."

"Precisely. You will be grounded until Bong has arrived in the United States. When I hear that he's got there safely, and that he's been feted at home as the leading ace, then I'll allow you to fly again and to fight. Don't you think that's a more sporting way of going on? Don't you think it's more elegant to take Bong's place as the leading ace than to pinch it from him?"

McGuire thought for few seconds.

"Yes, sir," he said, "you're right. But when will Bong be in the States?"

"He'll leave as soon as I have a place for him."

Richard Bong went home on a transport aircraft which took off at midnight on the 29th December, 1944, bound for San Francisco.

On the 6th January, General Kenney was informed of his arrival. Bong had been welcomed as was fitting: photographed, filmed and interviewed. The General invited McGuire to dinner and told him of this news.

"Bong has well deserved his success," said McGuire.

"And you have behaved very sportingly," said the General. "Now you have had enough rest. You can fly and fight. But take care! Don't get obsessed by this idea of beating the record or you are lost. If you try to force your luck it can abandon you. I don't want to have to write a letter to your parents one of these days. Keep calm and fight as though you hadn't a single victory to your credit."

"Yes, sir, you're right," replied McGuire, adding that two young recruits had just arrived in his squadron and that he was going to take them in hand.

"Major Rittmayer and myself will go with them. We'll carry out a little sweep over the Jap airfield. We'll see what sort of stuff these youngsters are made of. It will be a kind of instruction flight."

"That's fine," said the General. "Goodnight, McGuire."

On the following day at 7.45 hours the four pilots took off. They met a solitary Japanese aircraft above the Island of Negros at 2,000 feet.

"Follow me," said McGuire to the young pilot he had taken as his 'winger'.

He dived on the Japanese but the latter banked so abruptly that he was on the tail of Major Rittmayer's aircraft and began to machine-gun him. The Major cried over the intercom : "Give us a hand, McGuire !"

McGuire banked but his turn was so fantastically tight that his aircraft disintegrated. The wings ripped off and the machine hit the ground like a meteor. The Japanese fired a second burst at Rittmayer's aircraft which caught fire and crashed in turn. The Japanese was already speeding away at full speed and disappeared behind the hills. The two tyros did not even have time to interfere. The double tragedy had unfurled before their eyes in a few seconds. They could only return completely bewildered to their airfield and make their report. General Kenney had to write that letter to McGuire's parents.

The enemy had been conquered in Europe and the war continued against Japan. The American tide pushed the Japanese even further back towards their home islands from where they had launched the most gigantic offensive in history. Swarms of suicide pilots tried in vain to postpone the hour of disaster. As is known, the hour sounded on the 6th August, 1945, the day the white men, after some hesitation, decided for the first time to employ the apocalyptic bomb.

That day General Kenney's Air Force was at Okinawa. As soon as the news of the bomb explosion was known there was no other subject of conversation. Its existence had been suspected but no one had known anything definite.

"The tactics and art of warfare are going to be completely upset," said some of the pilots. "It will only need a handful of aircraft flying at very great altitudes carrying a few of these bombs."

Discussions started. In any case Japan's surrender was now imminent and the Second World War would certainly come to an end. Almost everyone was in agreement about this. An atmosphere of expectation began to replace the aggressive spirit.

Towards the end of the afternoon in all the huts of the Fifth Air Force no one spoke any more of the bomb. Another item of news had just come from the States, news which cast its gloom on every man's face.

Richard Bong had killed himself at Los Angeles on a training flight in a new jet fighter. Richard Bong, whom everyone believed to be out of danger, whom General Kenney had continued to keep out of the fighting zone because he was anxious for this rosy-faced fair-haired youth, who had once aroused his sympathy in his San Francisco office, to survive. Similar to his rival and friend, McGuire, Richard Bong had escaped all the Japanese bullets, only to lose his wings and plummet to the ground.

CHAPTER EIGHT

SWEDE LARSEN'S TEAM

In May, 1942, a group of a dozen pilots of the U.S. Navy were stationed on Norfolk Airfield, Virginia, which had recently been adapted to receive torpedo-carrying aircraft of a new type. These aircraft were T.B.F. Grumman Avengers, three-seater monoplanes equipped with a 1,600 h.p. engine, armed with two machine-guns firing through the propeller, two 50 mm. cannon in a revolving turret and a small 37 mm. cannon in the tail. They were gradually to replace the T.B.D. Douglas Devastators then in service, which were equipped with an engine of only 850 h.p. and were less well armed. The pilots detailed to receive the new aircraft had been detached from the carrier *Hornet*.

On the 30th May, Lietuenant Harold H. Larsen, known as "Swede", in command of this detachment, was sent for by Admiral Noyes.

"Orders," said the Admiral. "You will immediately detail your six pilots best familiar with the Grumman Avenger. They will take off tomorrow morning, destination Midway."

"Very good, sir," said Larsen. "I think I can put myself down among those six pilots."

"No, you'll have to remain here and continue training the others."

"But it would only be normal, sir," Larsen insisted, "if I were to go with my men if there's fighting to be done."

"I didn't say there would be any fighting. These aircraft have to go to Midway. That's all we know."

Admiral Noyes may have had some glimmer of what was happening at Midway or perhaps not. (The American Intelligence Service had decoded Japanese messages giving all the details of an imminent attack.) Nevertheless, it was easy to imagine that a priority order like this, sending six pilots with the most experience of the new torpedo-carrying aircraft to an advanced atoll position in the middle of the

Pacific, could not be a picnic.

While Larsen scrupulously selected his six pilots and their crews, he told himself that he was almost certainly choosing them for forthcoming battles in course of which these eighteen men would be exposed to the normal risks of wartime service. He had no idea that with the exception of two he was writing their death warrants. The six Grumman Avengers, after breaking their journey at Honolulu, landed on the eve of the 3rd June, at Midway. The following day at 08.12 hours all the members of their crews, with the exception of two, were dead.

The group of six TBFs from Norfolk had taken off from Midway at six in the morning to attack Japanese warships.

According to the Fighting Instructions of the U.S. Navy, squadrons of torpedo-carrying aircraft should not attack alone. Dive-bombers and fighters have to make the first attack on the enemy ships to put their anti-aircraft out of action and to deal with the enemy fighters. After this the torpedo-carrying aircraft attack escorted by fighters. This regulation tactic was devised because the torpedo-carrying aircraft is extremely vulnerable at the moment of attack. It has to launch its torpedo from close quarters if it is to have a chance of hitting a target which can manoeuvre as soon as it sees the wake of the torpedo. This aircraft can manoeuvre during its approach until the launching distance, but during this operation it has to remain for several seconds in a perfectly level flight. At this moment it is a sitting pigeon.

Now at Midway the six Grummans were the first to reach the enemy squadron (about 08.10 hours) alone and without escort. Admiral Nimitz's order was to hit the aircraft carriers at all costs. The latter sailed under the protection of fighters and surrounded by cruisers and destroyers. The Grummans came down to 120 feet and flew level among an extraordinarily dense crossfire of Japanese ack-ack. The Zeros buzzed around them like wasps, pursuing them rashly until they came into the field of fire of Japanese warships. Two minutes later five of the Grummans were shot down and their crews had been killed. The only Grumman to reach Midway was piloted by Ensign Albert K. Ernest with a dead man aboard – his rear-gunner who had been killed by Japanese bullets.

Other aircraft of the same unit (the Eight T.B.F. Group) also took part in the Battle of the Midway. The latter (15 Douglas Devastators) took off from the aircraft carrier *Hornet* and spotted the enemy about 09.20 hours. They, like the six Avengers, attacked on their own without escort and before any intervention by dive-bombers. The result was to be foreseen. The entire formation was wiped out. Not a single Devastator returned to land on the *Hornet*.

The only survivor was a Naval Ensign named George H. Gay, who managed to keep afloat on a cushion, refraining from blowing up his rubber dinghy before nightfall in order not to be spotted by the Japanese. He was thus present in the water at the ensuing Battle of Midway with a front seat view of the ensuing air attack with aircraft falling in the sea and ships sinking.

In brief, No. 8 Group of torpedo-carrying aircraft had lost sixty pilots out of sixty-three in the space of an hour and twelve minutes.

The news arrived a few days later in Norfolk, Virginia and was, of course, heard by Swede Larsen.

The group was reformed at Norfolk and sent, at the end of 1942, aboard the aircraft carrier *Saratoga*, a unit of one of the two powerful task forces (three aircraft carriers, a battleship, fourteen cruisers, thirty destroyers, ten auxiliary vessels, twenty-two transports) under the orders of Admirals Fletcher and Turner, to attack Guadalcanal.

Guadalcanal, 80 miles long and 35 miles wide, is a mountainous, jungle-covered island in the Solomons group. The Japanese had disembarked their troops and sappers in July, 1942, and had turned the plain which stretches along the northern shore of the island into an airfield. From the month of April, 1942, onwards the American High Command had decided to make the South-West Pacific an offensive zone. The first operation, therefore, was to chase the Japanese off Guadalcanal. The date for the attack which had been prepared in great detail was fixed for the 7th August, 1942.

The torpedo-carrying aircraft which took off that morning from the aircraft carriers carried no torpedoes but bombs. Their mission was to attack the Japanese installations of Guadalcanal and the neighbouring islands (Florida, Tulagi, Gavutu, Tananbogo), as well as the Japanese transports moored off shore.

The first thing that struck Swede Larsen and the other pilots was that the enemy they had been ordered to attack was completely invisible. Guadalcanal and the little islands appeared below their aircraft as impenetrable masses of tropical vegetation, separated by arms of empty sea. Here and there on a beach or in a clearing the airmen could see a few huts round which were clustered natives who waved to them in the friendliest manner.

By descending to a very low altitude they could finally spot the position and the Japanese dumps, remarkably camouflaged beneath the trees. Usually they had hardly discovered them when the anti-aircraft guns went into action. Then they had to fly off and run in again to drop their bombs on the target. A second later they were once more above impenetrable jungle. Sometimes a petrol dump went up in flames, cleaving this dark green expanse with huge flames.

The torpedo-carrying aircraft returned to their carrier to refuel and take on more ammunition before leaving once more for the jungle. The pilots, already less of novices, began to spot the camouflaged targets more easily. A cluster of palms on the shore would be a camouflaged tanker which a bomb could blow up.

The pilots had received orders to bomb with the maximum precision for contingents of marines had landed on the island and the atolls and were already engaged with the Japanese in the expanse of the jungle. But they had no idea of the violence and ferocity of the battles which were going on below, under the cover of the trees.

The following morning, 8th August, the pilots of No. 8 Group T.B.D. received orders to take off at the same time as No. 3 Group of dive-bombers (D.B.D. Douglas Dauntless with instructions to attack the caves on the island of Tananbogo).

"The Japanese have installed big guns in these caves,

147

covering the beach," the briefing officer explained. "The assault craft and the tanks have not yet been able to winkle them out for they are fighting like demons. The destroyer *Buchanan* sailed right in shore to attack these caves at close range but without result. You must attack at hedge-hopping level also at point-blank range. Naturally the Japs have plenty of ack-ack."

These T.B.D. pilots had never yet carried out a mission of this type but their normal routine had completely equipped them for a close range attack. Arriving above Tananbogo they saw several transports and assault craft which had been sunk. The most difficult thing was to discover the cave entrances in the flank of the hills which had to be bombed. As soon as they had spotted them, the pilots flew off and ran in to lay their eggs, zooming immediately to clear the top of the hill. Luckily none of them was shot down during this mission.

Three low-level air attacks and three tank attacks were necessary to reduce the defenders of Tananbogo hills, or rather to exterminate them. "The individual tenacity of the Japanese soldier was stupefying," wrote General Van de Grift in command of the 1st Division of Marines. "Each of them fought to the death, preferring suicide to surrender. In the course of the attack against the Solomon Islands, only three Japanese surrendered."

The American landing at Guadalcanal was carried out at comparatively moderate cost, for the enemy air opposition was rather weak. On the evening of the 8th August, the carriers which had supported the operation retired with the battleships, six cruisers and sixteen escorting destroyers, since the American High Command feared an attack by Japanese submarines. On the night of the 8th/9th, a force of Japanese cruisers and destroyers arrived out of the blue in the channel between Guadalcanal and the Isle of Savo and attacked Admiral Crutchley's cruisers which had been left behind. Four cruisers were sunk, one cruiser and two destroyers badly damaged. It was obvious that the Japanese had decided to hold on to Guadalcanal. In fact this island was to become a sort of Verdun of the Pacific.

On the 23rd August, 1942, Admiral Fletcher in command of the American squadron cruising south-east of Guadalcanal, received information that three Japanese aircraft carriers with their escorts had just been sighted south of Truk (Mariana Islands), steaming south-east. He set sail immediately to meet the enemy with his two aircraft carriers (*Saratoga* and *Enterprise*) escorted by a battleship, four cruisers and eleven destroyers.

Larsen's torpedo-carrying aircraft were airborne at the end of the afternoon, escorted this time by fighters and dive bombers. Unfortunately, when they arrived at the area indicated they did not see the enemy, despite a long search. Night fell and Larsen heard the order on his radio: "Don't try and reach the carrier tonight. Land at Guadalcanal on Henderson field and remain there until tomorrow morning."

As I have already said, this airfield (retaken from the Japanese) was on the north shore of Guadalcanal in the Lunga plain. The Americans had christened it after a pilot killed in the Battle of Midway. Larsen and his group found it quite easily in spite of the darkness. Shortly after they had sent out reconnaissance signals they saw lights go on on the ground, showing a flare path. The aircraft landed.

The pilots then realized that the flare path lights were simply rags dipped in petrol and set alight. On each side of the runway were aircraft, about a dozen in all, some of which looked in a piteous state. The camp was small and wretched, surrounded by coconut palms. The runway itself was rather like a bad road that has been hastily repaired. The new arrivals found themselves surrounded by haggard men who seemed in the last stages of exhaustion. They were pilots of the marine squadron based on Henderson field.

"Have you just come to spend the night?" they said. "It's a pity for us but so much the better for you. Anyhow, we'll give you some dinner."

The Mess was a rather low wooden hut and the dinner consisted of American tinned food, plus rice and fruit from captured Japanese stocks. The drink, which was also

Japanese, was a strange beverage in small bottles bearing the label "Hitsubi Champagne Cider".

As soon as dinner was over the marines showed their visitors to the dormitory, another wooden hut. The beds were stretchers, some of which had huge brown patches: the blood of dead comrades.

"The shelter trench is just over there," said the marines. "It's very practical."

Larsen and his pilots had just fallen asleep when the first shells began to fall on the airfield. They went into the shelter trench. "You're lucky," they said, "it doesn't seem to be very serious. It must be a submarine firing. There may be two of them."

The Japanese warships sailed close in shore every night to bombard the airfield and the other American positions. That night the shelling was not very severe and did not last long. The next morning the pilots left Henderson field for their aircraft carrier. They did not know that they would return to this sinister spot and would spend the darkest days of their lives there.

On the 24th contact was established with the Japanese fleet. No. 8 T.B.D. Group took off at 18.05 hours, this time in company with dive bombers and fighters. But when Larsen spotted the first Japanese vessel he also noticed that the dive-bombers and fighters were out of sight. They had probably been attracted to some other target.

The Japanese force consisted of ten cruisers surrounded by six destroyers. The carriers must have been some way off. *So much the worse*, thought Larsen, *we can always attack those.* The sun was on the point of sinking in the tropic sea in a magnificent blaze of purple. The Japanese ships looked like dark silhouettes dotted with red gleams from the flash of their ack-ack guns.

The T.B.D.s were now surrounded by a swarm of Zeros which began to fire on them. The Americans returned their fire and Larsen felt that some of the bullets had hit his aircraft. But he went on. He saw a destroyer just ahead, kept ten seconds in level flight to ensure a good launching and tripped the mechanism to free his torpedo. A few seconds later, when he had passed the Japanese force, he heard a voice in his headphones. "Good work, Swede, you hit it right in the guts. It's sinking."

Larsen set course for his carrier. He had a long distance to cover and he was now alone in the darkening sky above a sea the colour of a fish's belly. He connected his laryngophone to the intercom.

"Everyone okay aboard?" he asked.

"Okay, sir," replied the turret gunner.

"Okay, sir," replied the rear gunner.

Larsen felt a little relieved. He waited for a few seconds and then asked again. "Any of you guys see anything?"

No reply.

"Where are the others?" asked Larsen. "Where the hell are they?"

"I saw some aircraft crash, sir," said the turret gunner.

"How many? Japs or ours?"

"Two or three, sir. They hit the water, flaming like matches – perhaps four."

"But were they Japs or ours?"

"I don't know, sir."

As usual, they would only know when they returned to the carrier. Once the torpedo had gone, the routine was each man for himself.

A little later Larsen's aircraft was joined by two dive-bombers.

"How did it go?" he asked them on the radio.

In the dusk he saw that they replied by dipping their wings. He realized that they could hear but could not reply because their transmitters must be out of action. A little later the small group was joined by two aircraft of No. 8 Group T.B.D.s. Larsen asked them if they were all right. One of them replied "Okay" on the radio and the other dipped his wings. His transmitter, too, was out of action.

Night had now fallen but there was a moon. *That's a break*, thought Larsen. *It'll be easier to find the carrier.*

He switched his laryngophone over to long wave. Not a crackle to be heard. Larsen called his rear gunner; on board the T.B.F. the rear gunner was also in charge of transmitting.

"Why doesn't our long wave function?" asked Larsen.

"The set's been shot up, sir. Not a hope."

Larsen then called the T.B.F. whose wireless was functioning.

"My long wave's out of action. Try and get the carrier and ask for our course."

A few seconds later he heard a voice replying: "Sergeant Lawrence here. Our long wave spluttering. I can't get it going."

"You must try," said Larsen.

"I am trying, sir, but I can't do it."

"Eleven lives, including yours, depend on that radio."

"I know it, sir. I know it. I can't think of anything else."

Lawrence's voice was that of an exhausted and exasperated man. Larsen was a huge, fair-haired fellow whose nervous system seemed to stand up to any strain. But he was also a very understanding man.

"Well, let it alone for a while, Lawrence," he said. "We have a magnificent moon and perhaps we'll come across the carriers. Wouldn't it be something to take a bathe on one of those beaches on a night like this and with this sort of moon?"

A note of surprise crept into Sergeant Lawrence's voice.

"Yes, sir," he replied. "It certainly would be swell."

"Did you ever go bathing in South Carolina in the moonlight? They must be magnificent, the nights down there."

"You bet. And I've often bathed by moonlight."

"I was sure of it. Tell me about them."

Lawrence began to relate, at first rather hesitantly, and then more fluently as Larsen asked him the details.

The other airmen heard this extraordinary dialogue in the dark. At first they wondered what it was all about and if Swede Larsen had gone off his head. Then they understood. Their leader's marvellously calm voice worked on the Sergeant across the air. They heard his voice grow calmer too and when he had finished his story Larsen remained silent for a few seconds and said: "Well, Lawrence, what about trying to get that long wave set going again?"

Less than a minute later, Lawrence's voice cried: "It's working! It's working!"

In this way the group was able to ask a bearing from the carrier and finally to land.

Of the other T.B.D.s, some had been forced to land in various spots on the shores of Guadalcanal and the neighbouring islands but all the crews were safe. The Japanese had lost several warships, among them the aircraft carrier *Ryujo*.

At the beginning of September, the carriers having been sent back to the States for a refit, No. 8 Group T.B.D. were stationed in the New Hebrides. From this base they took part in several attacks against Japanese warships which were harassing the American lines of communication to Guadalcanal and bombarding their ground positions.

These attacks were carried out with the co-operation of dive-bombers and fighters. The result was that no machine from the group was shot down during this period. Both pilots and crews were very encouraged. They told each other every day that it was fine to do a good job in such superb conditions. It was at this time, at the end of September, that the group was transferred once more and received the order to instal itself on Henderson field.

It is hardly necessary to say that the situation had not improved there. The Japanese warships shelled Guadalcanal nearly every night. The defence troops on the island had finally christened the vessels which took part in this daily attack the "Tokyo Express". The Japanese force also brought up troops and material. By day the units hid from the American aircraft and remained along the banks under cover of jungle. At night they unloaded their cargo on Cape Hope, north of Guadalcanal. They advanced to the outskirts of the airfield, shelled and then retired at full speed.

Life on the airfield was no more pleasant during the day because Japanese bombers, escorted by Zeros, constantly attacked. As soon as the alarm was given, the T.B.D.s had to get into the air as quickly as possible and fly off, leaving a task of attacking the enemy and defending the airfield to the marine fighters.

No. 8 Group attacked either the Japanese warships with torpedoes or else bombed the troops which had been landed on Guadalcanal by the Tokyo Express.

On the 7th October, at nightfall, after carrying out one of these missions, Lieutenant John Taurman ran out of fuel near the island of San Cristobal near Guadalcanal. He landed his aircraft on the water and the three members of his crew – Taurman, Sergeants Bradley and Roback – hitched themselves without difficulty into their rubber dinghy while the aircraft sank.

Inside the dinghy were water and concentrated food tablets, and all they had to do was to wait calmly to be picked up. Several shipwrecked crews had been spotted and fished out of the water after several days.

About midnight the three men heard an aircraft fly overhead and by the sound of the engine they thought that it was an American. They decided to fire a flare. Unfortunately, hampered by the darkness, the flare pistol went off prematurely, ripping a hole in the bottom of the dinghy. The most serious thing was that their water and food were sunk.

The inflated walls of the dinghy still floated. The men straddled them, clinging on to this jury wheel to keep afloat.

"If the sharks come now," said one of them, "we've had our chips."

Luckily there were none, but the night breeze was icy cold. The men dived from time to time into the warm sea to restore circulation. At daybreak they saw that the shore was some way off. The shipwrecked men thought it better to wait for a rescue than to try and swim ashore, particularly as they noticed that the current was bearing them landwards. Their hearts were buoyed up with expectation but after midday – they were now suffering cruelly from the heat and thirst – this hope waned. Their raft was no longer approaching land but, on the contrary, was being carried further out to sea. By dusk, the airmen had returned almost to the spot where they had crashed.

The second night elapsed and half another day. The three men felt that their strength was ebbing and realized that soon they would not be able to cling on to this big rubber sausage.

"Well," said Sergeant Bradley, "I'm going to swim for it."

"The shore's a long way off," said his companions. "You'll be bushed before you get there and if your Mae West deflates you've had it."

"It won't deflate. Look, the current is obviously driving us in an ellipse, alternately carrying us near and far from the shore. There's no reason why that should ever stop. We shall go on round that ellipse until we're dead and our skeletons will continue in the same orbit like the planets. I'm going to swim for the shore." His mates were too exhausted to continue the discussion.

"Don't worry yourselves," he said, as he swam off. "I'll bring you relief and a case of iced beer."

Bradley began to swim across the current and noticed to his delight that he was making headway. But a little later he realized that he, too, was being carried along in the ellipse.

He felt as though someone had hit him on the head. For one moment he thought of returning to his comrades so as not to die on his own at least. Then he pulled himself together and decided to stick it out.

He continued to swim towards the shore and sometimes had the impression that it was drawing nearer. But soon it became remote again. Bradley swam and then had to give up from exhaustion. Night came and he could no longer see the coast. He abandoned the struggle and floated like a corpse.

He was still alive the following morning, and saw to his joy that the shore was now quite near. He managed to swim feebly. The shore drew closer and now his own speed increased. He was going faster than an exhausted swimmer could possibly have done. He realized that he had managed to leave the elliptic current and that another current had caught him and was bearing him towards the land.

Some natives found him on a beach, his skin peeled by the sun and the salt water, covered with scratches received as he was dragged over a coral reef. The natives looked after him as best they could and went out in their canoes to find the other men. But they found nothing. The following day Bradley was brought back to Guadalcanal by an American aircraft and evacuated. Lieutenant Taurman and Sergeant Roback were never discovered, although a search was made for several days.

In spite of all American efforts the Japanese had managed to land a division on Guadalcanal. Life at Henderson field was hell. Each time the airmen returned from their attacks on the warships or the Japanese positions, they found the airfield more damaged.

For lack of staff they had to refuel their own aircraft or, to be more accurate, to go and fetch fuel from trucks captured from the Japanese. These jerry cans of petrol were on the landing beaches. They had to unload them – each one weighed 370 lb. – and pump the fuel into the aircraft. For lack of material they had to drag the bombs and torpedoes on improvised trolleys; the spare parts they needed were taken from damaged aircraft. If an alert sounded they had to make a whirlwind take-off. Sometimes they had no time to take off, and could only run to the trenches while the bombs were falling.

No sleep at night. During the shelling by the Tokyo Express (the force was always different but generally included a few destroyers and one or two cruisers) the men counted the firing detonations and waited for the corresponding number of explosions. These night bombardments were more exhausting than their air fights. No. 8 Group Mess consisted of a few small tents planted under the palm trees on a soil which the rain transformed into a morass. Most of the airmen succumbed to malaria and dysentry.

The Tokyo Express which sailed inshore towards Guadalcanal on the night of the 12th October, comprised two battleships, a cruiser and eight destroyers. The bombardment of Henderson field that night surpassed anything that the defenders of Guadalcanal, including the most hardened marines, had ever undergone or imagined.

The noise of the salvoes seemed like the roar of several trains in a tunnel. Twenty seconds elapsed between this noise and the explosions. After the explosion they could hear the whine of falling sharpnel.

The airmen of No. 8 Group were lying flat in the bottom of foxholes dug round their little tents. From time to time there was a few minutes lull, then the night was broken by the screams of the wounded or perhaps of men who were already half demented.

At dawn, when the shelling ceased, the inhabitants of the airfield climbed out of their holes. Their eyes met greenish haggard faces beneath a several days' growth of beard. This appalling non-stop bombardment, however, had killed only eight men and wounded eighteen on the airfield. On the other hand all their aircraft had been destroyed except three which might possibly fly "another day".

That morning Larsen received orders by radio to evacuate his aircraft. At that moment none of them was airworthy. The marines on Guadalcanal were digging new trenches and a land attack on the airfield seemed imminent.

"There's no question now of pulling out," said Larsen. "We might just as well fight on land with the marines."

With the exception of two pilots and two mechanics who remained on Henderson field to try to repair the two damaged machines, the airmen of No. 8 Group were given guns and hand-grenades and joined the troops. The front line consisted of a certain number of foxholes dug in the jungle, from which each day the marines charged other holes held by Japanese at moments when they were not obliged to defend themselves against attack.

The enemy was nearly always invisible. There were sudden shots from little yellow men perched like monkeys in the trees; they had remained there motionless for hours waiting for a good target. At night the jungle echoed with the cries of wild beasts, the scream of Japanese looming suddenly out of the dark, whistles, rifle and machine-gun shots. A repulsive stench of corruption hung in the air.

On the 20th October, Larsen was told that the first aircraft was ready. It had been assembled with the wings of one machine, the engine of another, and the fuselage of a third. Some of the pilots said: "It'll never fly."

Larsen tested it and it flew. On the following day, two more aircraft were ready. With the aid of these three jerry-built flying machines the airmen of No. 8 Group carried out an attack on a Japanese position and set fire to an ammunition dump. In the course of this operation, Larsen's aircraft was hit by anti-aircraft and had to land on a beach. The crew returned to Henderson field through the jungle.

On the morning of the 25th October, the Tokyo Express returned and landed troops and material at Cape Hope. The shelling that night was even more terrible than it had been on the 12th October. Later in the day, Japanese tanks attacked. The American front was broken and the Japanese assault troops captured part of the airfield.

At dawn the battle developed into hand-to-hand fighting between small groups of exhausted men. Some of the American combatants were in a state of nerves approaching despair. But the Japanese resistance had been no less tested. They staggered forward and were mowed down by machine-gun fire.

During the day General Van de Grift shortened his front, made a rousing speech to his troops and launched a counter-attack led by a regiment of marines. The Japanese did not give a yard of ground. The 2,200 which held the aerodrome were finally exterminated on the spot. Henderson field, the key position of Guadalcanal had been re-conquered.

The airmen of No. 8 Group began to look among the wrecked aircraft for parts that could be used. On the 7th November, three machines were once more airworthy. All Larsen's crews took part that day in an attack against Japanese warships, hitting and sinking a cruiser.

At last on the 13th November, 1942, Larsen received definite orders: the survivors of No. 8 Group were to be relieved and replaced by another unit. Now the fate of Guadalcanal was no longer in the balance. The Japanese re-embarked their troops and material and retired under the assault of the American Air Force and Navy. The hell of Guadalcanal was over.

Larsen and his group left the island on the 15th November. A few days later they were at Honolulu being interviewed by a radio reporter. They felt that they had arrived from another world. They could find no words to describe this world of jungle, misery, death and corruption. It now seemed to them a hideous nightmare.

"At least say a few words to your families who are listening in."

The reporter handed them the microphone. One after the other they uttered a few, rather clumsy and commonplace phrases: "Yes, it's been pretty tough." "The Japs held on like limpets but we beat them in the end." Yes, they were very pleased to be going on leave. They were thinking of their "buddies" who would not return.

Several of these men were to take part in other murderous battles in the course of the Pacific war and some of them were not to return. For all those who survived until the end, the most impressive word of the war remained that Melanesian name with the magic syllables: Guadalcanal.

CHAPTER NINE

IVAN KOJEDOUB AND THE
NORMANDIE-NIEMAN REGIMENT

"When Kojedoub paid us a visit," the survivor said to me, "he had not yet reached his score of 62 victories and our unit was only called the Normandie. But that is important. Don't quote my name for it's quite useless. I only want to talk to you today of the Normandie-Niemen as a team, as a group of exiles fighting in a country which has nothing in common with our own. But, first of all, as regards Ivan Kojedoub. . . ."

I think that it will be more entertaining to the reader if I act merely as a stenographer and record the words of this survivor.

I cannot remember the exact number of victories Kojedoub had to his credit at that period. It was in the autumn of 1943, but it was high enough to impress us. When he arrived with his "winger" Titarenko, several of our men were scrapping with some Messerschmitt 110s in the immediate neighbourhood. Kojedoub and Titarenko plunged into the fight and shot down two enemy aircraft just over our airfield. Then they landed and came and shook hands with us.

For Kojedoub nothing in the world was more natural than to shoot down Messerschmitt 110s. His very appearance gave one an impression of extraordinary power, one might almost say of invulnerability. You know how robust Russians are when they are well built.

Kojedoub had just given us a display on his Lavotchkine 7 fighter-bomber and he also flew a Yak to demonstrate how he attacked German aircraft at low altitudes. Of course this was of great interest to me but Kojedoub's personality really intrigued me. I finally had a long chat with him which was almost in the nature of an interview.

This conversation was arranged by our liaison officer, the political commissar, Lieutenant Kounine, for like most of us I knew very little Russian. Since I realized that Lieutenant Kounine was to be present at this conversation, I simply asked Ivan Kojedoub to tell me his life story. This made him laugh a great deal at the start but when I insisted and he began to speak, Kounine translated.

The tale of his childhood seemed to come out of one of those Russian fairy picture books. He was born in 1920 in a Ukrainian village called Obrajevka. I made a note of this name. It was a village where people spoke a dialect half Russian, half Ukrainian. His father apparently worked in a factory some distance away and the family was very poor. ...

At that moment Lieutenant Kounine interrupted to explain to me that in 1920 the Soviet Regime had only just come to power and had not yet had time to improve the living conditions of the population.

In the winter little Ivan went with his father to a neighbouring forest to collect faggots. "He cut the dry branches and I carried them home in the sleigh. I loved pulling the sleigh." Kojedoub spoke almost nostalgically and with a rather touching sentimentality of nature, the forest in the snow, his village and the seasonal changes in the Ukraine. No peasant in the world loves his land so much as the Russian.

Ivan learned to read in his playtime from the labels on grocery packets. This did not surprise me. I only had to look at his face, his eyes and the shape of his head to realize that inside it there was a brain which had always functioned rapidly and efficiently. He entered the village school at the age of six but his father soon took him away and found him a job with a shepherd in a neighbouring village. But the boy left the sheep and returned home saying: "I want to go on with my schooling." His intellectual curiosity got the better of his love of nature.

Another vocation manifested itself later and Ivan Kojedoub might quite easily have become a painter instead of an airman, for he had a great talent for drawing. A certain Malychok, who exhibited his pictures in the village cultural club (the regime's great didactic effort had begun to make itself felt) had spotted young Ivan's gift and given him lessons. Unfortunately Malychok fell ill shortly afterwards and died. "I did not become a painter," said Kojedoub, "but his lessons helped me to acquire a great visual memory and a spirit of observation. These qualities have been very useful to me since I became a pilot."

As a youth he made friends with boys who frequented a flying club. The creation of these clubs was also part of the great Soviet effort. "I decided to join too," he said. "At that time I had just read Tchkalov's book on his crossing of the North Pole. This exploit by the great Soviet airman made a great impression on me. I applied to enter the flying school and was admitted in January, 1938."

In principle the doors of nearly every career are open to all young Russians who are ambitious and eager to learn, but the conditions for study are difficult, selection is severe and those who fail in their first exams fall back into the masses from where they have little chance of emerging in the future. Fortunately for him, Ivan Kojedoub had an intelligence, a memory and a will power which were far above the ordinary. Moreover, as I have said, his physical strength was outstanding. Thus he passed the first stage in his flying instruction without the least difficulty.

At the beginning of 1940, he was admitted to a fighter school. He shone there to such an extent that at the end of the course he was made an instructor. "I had eleven pupils which seemed to me extraordinary. A few months before I had been a pupil with them and now I was given men whom I had to teach to fly a fighter aircraft. I had to understand their individual characters, mentalities and capacities. That interested me a great deal."

As you see, Kojedoub already possessed teaching capabilities.

"As I gave my instruction I continued to learn myself and I prepared each lesson very seriously. I wanted to have everything perfect so as not to lose my authority, in fact all my movements were carried out with the precision of an automaton."

You know that Germany attacked the U.S.S.R. on the 22nd June, 1941. Ivan Kojedoub, however, remained an instructor. It was not until November, 1942, that he was sent to a fighter regiment and given a Lavotchkine – an La 5. He practised formation flying which he had not yet learned. Russian pilots were given an extremely long period of training. Everything goes very slowly in Russia. A human specimen like Kojedoub must have assimilated any instruction very quickly, but all his comrades were not of the same ilk.

"When did you at last fight against the enemy?" I asked.

"In March this year."

"Tell me about your first combat."

"Well, it was like this. I was on my own on patrol and suddenly below me I saw aircraft dropping bombs on our airfield. They were Messerschmitts 109s."*

My heart beat faster.

"I can hardly believe it," I said.

"Yes, there were six of them and I was alone. I had sworn to myself that I would shoot down an enemy in my first sight. I must attack at least two of them, I thought.

But at that moment I remembered the rule which had been drummed into our heads: *Before attacking, look behind you.* I turned my head for a fraction of a second and saw a Messerschmitt on my tail. The next moment a few bullets hit my left wing. Then four other Messerschmitts attacked me, hitting me in the wings and the fuselage. My aircraft, riddled with holes, would hardly stay in the air. Not only had I failed to shoot down a single enemy aircraft but I had not even had time to attack. I could have baled out but I wanted at all costs to land and save my machine. I now felt completely calm. I managed to land and immediately got out of my machine. The Commander of the regiment was Soldatenko. 'Don't worry,' he said, 'that's your baptism. You mustn't think it's so easy to shoot down a plane. We'll study your flight and your landing. It will teach you a lesson.' You see it was not very brilliant."

"Well, you've made up for lost ground since then," I

* Messerschmitt 109s were employed as semi-dive bombers on the Russian Front.

said. "As far as I have been able to learn of your victories, you seem to be able to hit your opponent any moment you choose. ...."

"You must never lose your head or get excited," said Kojedoub. "You have to act very quickly and at the same time calculate each movement. But you have to have enthusiasm too."

"Enthusiasm?"

"Yes, because it excites the mind and keeps you on the alert. It also prevents you feeling your expenditure of energy."

"I don't think you have much to worry about in that respect."

"It's true I'm very strong physically," said Kojedoub, "but like everyone else, as soon as I'm on the ground I realize my loss of nervous energy. You know as well as I do that you use up more in a quarter of an hour's aerial combat than you do during a week on the ground. That is why it's always necessary to leave for a fight in perfect physical trim."

Ivan also spoke to me about the evenings spent in the Soviet Air Messes. "We discuss all sorts of technical questions, group flying, fighting tactics, the risks that are justified and those one must avoid. We spend every evening together perfecting our tactics."

Actually we knew that the Russian airmen spent many roisterous evenings but it is almost certain that most of them were fanatically interested in their profession and that like all Soviet Russians they had a taste for dialectic. Kojedoub was probably a kind of Stakhanovite among fighters. He described several more of his air battles, constantly repeating that the main thing was "To calculate each moment and at the same time to have plenty of audacity." Obviously. The difficulty consists in putting this principle into action.

The story of Ivan Kojedoub's exploits has been published in several Russian papers. In November, 1943, he was sent to rest and then once more to the front in the Kirovgrad sector. On 4th February, 1944, he was made Hero of the Soviet Union and a few days later received the

Gold Star. In May, 1944, his score stood at 45 official victories.

After this he was given command of the Byelo-Russian air front while retaining his command of a group. His qualities as a leader seem to have been no less remarkable than his qualities as a fighter. I think that everything must have been easy for this wild man of the wood who, at the same time, was a superiorly organized machine. He took part in the air battles over Germany right to Berlin. At the end of the war, having reached his record of 62 official victories, he was named for the third time Hero of the Soviet Union.

"A few days later," Ivan Kojedoub wrote, "I left for my native village of Obrajevka. I was expected. The whole village had turned out and I was asked to say a few words. I was terribly moved. I spoke of my country, of the love we bore it and of my comrades and related a few of my combats.

"I visited my parents' tombs. I thought of my father who was so proud of my boyhood drawings and my early success as an airman. How happy he would have been to see me now! I remained for a few days in the village and then, after saying my solemn farewells, I left for Moscow. It is six years since I flew for the first time and now my life is dedicated to aviation. I shall continue to perfect my technique and to acquire further knowledge. A long life lies ahead of me."

Another Russian story-book picture as you can see, but which is no fiction. In reading these lines I can still see the powerful frame and the well-balanced face of this in-vulnerable airman. I could see Ivan Kojedoub's return to his Ukraine village and imagine the little crowd of villagers intimidated at first by the hero who had been given the greatest official honours, then finding under this glorious uniform, Ivan, the boy from their village, who spoke their dialect, who had been on the school benches and played with so many of them. It must have been a touching cere-mony and the farewells must have been even more poig-nant. I do not know where Ivan Kojedoub is now, nor what he is doing. There was certainly a trace of official propaganda in those last lines. "I shall continue to perfect my technique and to acquire further knowledge." But when he wrote them I am sure Ivan Kojedoub was not lying. I cannot imagine the day when he will cease to want to go forward.

What shall I tell you now of Normandie-Niemen? In actual fact everything can be found in the regiment's log book – after operating as a group we became a regiment to conform with the Soviet Air Force units – and Roger Sauvage, one of the aces of the team, has described various episodes in the liveliest possible manner in his book *Un du Normandie-Niemen*. It is true that he only arrived in the regiment in January, 1944, after our first two Russian campaigns. The log book today is out of print and impossible to obtain.* Moreover, when I say that everything can be found in it, this is not strictly true. The log book contains the daily record of ops, combats, victories and losses and some details are lacking even about the inner life of the group. But I understand now in retrospect that these pages only partially give an account of the exhausting reality which this long adventure was for us.

4,354 war flying hours, 869 air battles, 273 enemy aircraft shot down and 46 killed or missing: these are the figures. But what cannot be translated into figures is the feeling of exile, cold, dust and heat, the wretched discomfort which we suffered almost everywhere after our combats.

On return from ops, airmen who fought with the R.A.F. – at least those who were in Great Britain – could relax in well heated, well lit messes and sleep in clean beds. We had to fight against bed bugs. They attacked us sometimes so furiously that we preferred to sleep outside on the ground in flea bags. There was nothing to be done about this and the Russians fought in the same conditions. You must realize that for most of the time we arrived on airfields which the Russian troops had just captured and which we ourselves had attacked some weeks before. As

* *Histoire de l'escadrille Normandie-Niemen*, journal de marche. Office français d'éditions.

the troops advanced we left the base which had just been improved to land on another.

For example, I remember arriving at Ivanovno airfield near Moscow on the 2nd December, 1942. Some of us had come from Syria and some from England via Lagos. The Russian cold greeted us. 35° C. below. And we saw Russian mechanics working with their bare hands. The earth was frozen six feet below the surface. We were equipped with fur bonnets and felt boots. Major Tulasne said to me: "I'm giving you two months' training. We shall be flying Yaks."

This training started on Yak 7s, which were biplanes. Then we were given monoplanes, Yaks 1, 3 and 9. The first time we saw them we thought they were toys. They were of wood and very lightly built, but we were soon to appreciate their handiness. They took off in 750 yards, climbed better than a Focke-Wulf and were easier to fly than a Dewoitine 520.

The day a Russian general came to watch our final training on the Yak 1 – this was at the beginning of March, 1943 – several of us did a complete circuit in eighteen seconds. A circuit in 25 seconds was considered a good performance by the Russians. This is merely to show that we were very strictly trained.

We flew our first missions at the front by the end of March. Our job was mainly to escort bombers. The chief difficulty came from the condition of our airfield which, in places, was like a lake of mud, ice and snow. In Russia the thaw is almost as terrible as the cold.

I do not think that any of us will forget the date of our first victory as a group: 5th April, 1943. That day Lieutenant Preziosi shot down a Focke-Wulf. A month later the score was at seven but we had lost four men.

The group was then transferred to another airfield at Kationki. The heat and the dust had replaced the mud. The pilots slept in a village two miles from the airfield with the exception of the C.O., Major Tulasne, who slept in a log-roofed shelter on the airfield, twenty yards from his aircraft.

Tulasne was a remarkable leader – intelligent, resolute

and kindly. He had passed through Saint Cyr and came from an army family. He had been in command of a fighter group in Tunisia and then in Syria from where he escaped. On the 17th July, 1943, he had two Focke-Wulfs shot down on the Russian front to his credit. He was decorated with the Soviet Order of the War for the Fatherland. That day, the 17th July, he took off at the head of a patrol of nine Yaks to escort the Russian fighter-bombers. Over the lines the formation met about thirty FWs and Tulasne disappeared in the course of the ensuing combat. We saw him for the last time losing height, then his aircraft was lost to sight in the swirling melée. We never had any news of him and his body was never found.

Major Pouyade took over command of the group. Preziosis, the man to open our score, disappeared a few days later in similar circumstances to Tulasne.

We frequently changed airfields and were migratory birds on the immense Russian steppe. On our return from each mission we wondered who would be missing at roll call.

Sometimes, unfortunately only too rarely, someone who was missing in the evening reappeared the following day or several days later. He would tell us how he had baled out or made a crash landing with a damaged aircraft in the middle of the battle. These stories began to give us some idea of the terrible violence of the fighting on the Russian front. The troops entered villages where corpses were piled up among gutted and burnt out vehicles, leaving an appalling stench of dead bodies in the air.

By the middle of September we had shot down about fifty enemy aircraft but our effectives were reduced to eighteen pilots, only five of whom had arrived with the first contingent. At this moment began the famous offensive against Smolensk in which we participated to cover the Russian advance.

Smolensk fell on the 25th September. The Russians laid on great celebrations while we did our best to fight against the bed bugs. In the middle of October, the division telephoned group to say that we should not be called upon for any more missions until further orders because there were too few of us and we were too war-weary. We took up winter quarters at Tula, 175 miles from Moscow.

At Tula we were quartered in a new airfield building. No more bed bugs – what a joy! We were invited to dances in the Red Army local and danced with charming young Russian girls. This was a change after the peasant girls with huge legs and enormous arms. We spent Christmas in Moscow and went to performances at the Bolshoi Theatre, a gigantic opera house overladen with gilt and statues.

Did I go on the Moscow Underground? Naturally. The stations are vast, with many-coloured mosaics. When the train enters, an absolutely terrifying flood of Muscovites in cloaks, steaming with damp, leap from the carriages and the crowd on the platform rushes for the doors. The French Métro even in the worst rush hours offers nothing to compare with this sight. Nothing in Russia is on the same scale as in France.

We remained at Tula, where the newly-arrived pilots were being trained to fly Yaks, until the middle of May. The group was then transformed into a regiment and sent to Doubrovka, fifteen miles from the front line. There we were back again to the old discomfort ... and the bed bugs.

On the morning of the 25th May, 1944, those whom these insects had not prevented from sleeping were woken up by a thunderous growl which shook the *isbas*: the new Russian offensive had begun.

The Red Army advanced 150 miles in five days in a tropical heat. We covered the advance and fought above it. About the middle of July, when we changed airfields once more, we lost one of the best in our group in the following manner.

Those who had already landed on the new airfield – it was at Mikoutani south of Vilno in Lithuania – were waiting for the others. We saw Captain de Seynes' aircraft coming in and all of us had a presentiment that a tragedy was about to take place. The aircraft was smoking and short flames were spouting from it.

Will he make it? we wondered. We saw the Yak speed

across the airfield, sway, climb again, return, zoom once more. This happened three times. Seynes must have been terribly intoxicated by the petrol fumes, or else blinded. Major Pouyade rushed to the radio and cried: "Bale out, Seynes." The captain was then at 1,500 feet and had height enough to jump. But no, he tried once more to land. This time the aircraft stalled and crashed.

Inside the wreck we found not one, but two corpses – Maurice de Seynes in the pilot's seat and behind him his Russian mechanic Biezoloub.

The body of the Yak allowed a passenger to be carried without a parachute. To reach this new airfield, Seynes had taken his faithful mechanic who was attached to him with a doglike devotion. A leaky pipe had set the aircraft on fire. Seynes had refused to jump so as not to abandon the wretched Biezoloub to his death, since the mechanic could not have jumped. Several of us wept.

At Mikoutani we were stationed in a farm house. We still slept in the open air because of the bugs but we were delighted to see brick houses, trees and undulating fields. At last we had left the endless Russian plain with its *isbas* and found ourselves once more in a European landscape. The town even possessed a bookshop. We took a few days off and went duck shooting. We bartered with the inhabitants because the rouble had no official value in the region. For a shirt we could get eight chickens.

And the war went on. After a comparatively calm summer – we were still carrying out bomber escort and ground attacks on German troops, although the enemy air activity seemed to have slowed down – we were plunged into the furnace of an offensive against East Prussia.

This was perhaps our most terrible ordeal. I think I must quote here one or two of the figures which can be found in the log book.

16th October. 100 missions. 29 of the enemy shot down.
17th October. 109 missions. 12 aircraft shot down.
18th October. 88 missions. 12 aircraft shot down.
20th October. 71 missions. 11 aircraft shot down.
22nd October. 56 missions. 14 aircraft shot down.
23rd October. 56 missions. 9 aircraft shot down.

Our activity and our victories continued in this rhythm until the end of the month. During this period we only lost two of our men. Naturally this was two too many, for you realize that each new loss affected us as much as the former ones. But taking into account the number and the violence of the combats a loss of two was very small.

Then the bad weather returned and we flew less often. At the end of November, Lieutenant Roland de la Poype was proclaimed Hero of the Soviet Union. Other pilots were to receive this honour later. This was also the period that Stalin gave the regiment the name of Normandie-Niemen as a reward for its exploits.

At the beginning of December we returned to Moscow – two days in the train – where we were presented to General de Gaulle and received decorations. The survivors of the original contingent were sent back to France and Major Delfino replaced Major Pouyade as officer commanding the regiment.

A few pictures still come to my mind. I remember, for example, a visit to a strange village near Vilno in Lithuania. The people who lived there were of the purest Mongolian type. We learned that it was an oasis which had lost nothing of its original character since a 15th century invasion. And these Mongolians were Mohammedans. In the village there was a mosque and a muezzin who invoked Allah from the top of the minaret. The villagers all spoke Polish or Russian but some of them read the Koran in Arabic.

And I can still see that column of camels dragging *telegas* near Kaunas. Camels, yes; you must never be surprised in Russia !

With the departure of the "old hands" a page came to an end in the history of Normandie-Niemen, but the war was not yet finished for the regiment. It was to participate in the 1945 campaign in Germany. This offensive began in the middle of winter, on the 13th January of that year.

In the west the allied troops had reached the frontiers of the Reich and final victory was only a matter of time. And yet, on certain days, the airmen of Normandie-Niemen had the impression that this war would never finish. From one snow-covered airfield to another, the migratory birds continued their battles. They were now at grips with the German aces of Mölders' group – the noses of their aircraft bore an ace of spades – nothing but officer pilots fanatically defending their doomed country.

Once more the Normandie-Niemen regiment was reduced to twenty-five pilots. Those who baled out landed on battlefields literally covered with German and Russian dead. They had to wade through corpses. One of the pilots fell into the sea at Frischeshafen, 800 yards from the shore. He managed to swim to a kind of hulk, a mere couple of planks to which he clung. From eleven in the morning until midnight the Russians and Germans fighting on the shore fired on him alternatively with rifles, machine-guns and even with cannon. He had to dive into the sea to avoid the projectiles. During the night, swimming as best he could and still clinging on to his hulk – he was wounded in the right leg – he contrived to reach the shore. He arrived in no man's land in the middle of an attack and fainted just as the Russian assault waves arrived. He was finally picked up by the Russians, brought back to life in a shelter, and evacuated under fire. From the hospital to which he had been transported he wrote a letter to Major Delfino which ended: "Bring me shoes, socks, a pair of trousers and a battledress. I haven't a stitch left. How good it is to be alive."

The most amazing spectacle of the war greeted the eyes of the Normandie-Niemen pilots on the 8th April, 1945, the day they participated as a fighter escort in the bombing of Koenigsberg. The town, over which hundreds of bombers flew with their escorts, was a single furnace. The *Katchukas*, incendiary jet shells, fell on the few parts of the town that had been spared by the bombers.

Koenigsberg capitulated after three days infernal struggle. The following day the German artillery in retreat shelled the airfield where the Normandie-Niemen aircraft had landed. Pilots and mechanics had to take refuge in trenches where, a few days earlier, Germans had also sheltered. The following day they were in the air again.

Between their flights above the harassed, strafed and decimated enemy troops the pilots visited the ruins of German cities which had been conquered. People with old men, women and terrified children. ... The bombing had been succeeded by the entry of Soviet shock troops. We know what they mean. This aspect of the war was indubitably the most tragic.

The Russian and American troops joined up at Torgau on the 27th April, 1945. The 8th May, the day on which hostilities ceased officially, an order from the Russian Command arrived at the Normandie-Niemen headquarters: "Lieutenant-Colonel Delfino will report immediately with his Yak in Warsaw where he will board a Douglas for Moscow to arrange formalities for the repatriation of French pilots."

It takes a long time to acclimatize yourself to the idea of surviving. The sentiment of peace does not explode like a flare among senses hardened by the war. The pilots of Normandie-Niemen heard this word repatriation as though it had come to them from another planet. They had not yet left their tragic, wretched, wartime world.

A few days in Moscow brought them some relaxation. On a special order from Stalin these pilots were to return to France in their war aircraft and each one of them would keep his Yak as a personal present – the war hatchet received as a magnificent souvenir from the Great Chief.

The pilots actually returned to France in their Yaks by stages: Posen, Prague, Stuttgart, Saint-Dizier. They skimmed over the rooftops of the Champs-Elysées and landed at Le Bourget. The Ministre de l'Air and two generals were waiting for them, accompanied by Mr. Bogomolov, the Soviet Ambassador in France. We were congratulated and decorated but were not allowed to keep our souvenir aircraft. But we possessed other imperishable souvenirs in our memories. The pilots of Normandie-Niemen realized at last that their long adventure was really at an end.

CHAPTER TEN

VOLUNTEERS FOR DEATH

THE special formation of four Zeros detached from No. 1 Air Squadron and placed under the command of Lieutenant Yuhiho Seki, arrived above the Gulf of Leyte in the Philippines, flying at 9,000 feet, about 07.45 hours on the 25th October, 1944. Each time his aircraft came out of a cloud, Yuhiho Seki saw below him American ships like motionless toys on the grey-blue surface of the sea. At the edge of the Gulf, close to the thin line of white foam which outlined the coast was a host of transports, small escort vessels and landing craft. Further off-shore a number of destroyers and aircraft carriers. . . .

Yuhiho Seki regretted that he could not see among them any of those gigantic flying decks of which he had dreamed. Below him now there were only escort aircraft carriers; the big ones must have been elsewhere. However, these were quite interesting targets. If each of the four Zeros managed to sink one – why not, after all, by using the new method? – it would be a considerable blow to the American naval forces. And other special formations would attack the big aircraft carriers at a later date. The important thing was to inaugurate the new system of attack, to prove its absolute efficiency.

The leading Zero was now almost directly above the group of aircraft carriers furthest removed from the shore. Seki glanced behind him. His three comrades were following. The moment for action had arrived. He dipped his wings and noticed that the other returned his salute. Pushing his stick forward he dived on the centre aircraft carrier.

The surface of the sea hollowed like a pail while the ship seemed to disperse outwards. The platform of the centre aircraft carrier grew larger and Yuhiho Seki could see the aircraft parked in the stern. He increased the angle of dive. The Zero carried a 500 lb. bomb beneath its belly.

He was now at a height at which the bomb could have been dropped with accuracy but he did not touch the release mechanism. He made no gesture and was content to keep the joystick pushed right forward, shaken by the terrible vibration of his aircraft as it dived like a meteor. With wide-open eyes, watching his target grow in size – the deck of this aircraft carrier which was to be his last picture of the visible world. Possibly other images flashed across his mind at this terrifying speed during those fractions of a second but no one will ever know. Yuhiho Seki perhaps had time to see the American sailors running along the deck and others falling on their bellies. Then there was the deafening, blinding explosion. Lieutenant Yuhiho Seki had voluntarily crossed the mortal frontier of which we know nothing.

The American aircraft carrier was the *Santee*. The anti-aircraft had not had time to open fire nor had the vessel a chance of taking avoiding action. Almost simultaneously the crew heard the explosion on the arrival of the meteor and then other explosions. Petrol tanks and ammunition blew up. A group of aircraft burst into flames.

And already two other Zeros were diving on the neighbouring aircraft carriers. The ack-ack from these ships opened fire and both aircraft were hit. They exploded in the water short of their targets.

The fourth Japanese had delayed his dive. The sailors had seen him circling in the sky as though he wanted to observe his companions' actions, or perhaps the pilot was hesitant. The ack-ack opened fire. A shell must have hit the machine, for a long trail of black smoke issued from it. Then the pilot made up his mind. He dived on the aircraft carrier *Swanee* and the gunners could not stop him. From all the vessels of the flotilla they heard the shock and saw the flames. The fourth Japanese had also dived on his target without releasing his bomb. He had exploded with it.

A second, similar attack, launched by six aircraft – suicide aircraft, the American sailors called them – took place at eleven o'clock. Two of the attackers, hit in their descent, fell into the sea. Another exploded on a level with the flying deck of its target, so near that the bloody human remains were spattered over the men. Three hit the target, damaging an aircraft carrier and sinking another, the *Saint-Lo*.

A dozen more suicide aircraft attacked American shipping in the Gulf of Leyte on the following morning, 26th October. They arrived above the clouds and began to describe large circles like birds of prey. The pilots then chose their victims or granted themselves a last meditation before deciding to start their death dive. The American sailors, in any case, were no longer in doubt as to their intentions. The gunners knew what they risked if they did not manage to destroy these madmen before they crashed. In the course of the suicide aircraft attacks of the 25th and 26th October, 1944, one escort carrier was sunk, four seriously damaged, and a host of American sailors killed or wounded. (On board the *Swanee* there were 85 killed, 58 missing and 92 wounded). Twenty Japanese pilots had deliberately sacrificed their lives to obtain these results.

The press and the American broadcasting stations at the time tried to make it appear that these suicide attacks cost the enemy a great deal for insignificant results. We shall examine the truth of this. In any case the American sailors at the outset were extremely impressed by this new mode of attack. Each time they realized that the Zero diving on their ship was piloted by one of these volunteers for death, they felt strangely ill at ease. They understood facing an enemy who was resolved to fight to the death. But it was a different matter to be attacked by an enemy who deliberately and systematically killed himself in order to kill you. This type of combat introduced a new psychological element into the war which was difficult for the occidental mind to accept.

At the end of the 13th century the Mongol conqueror, Kublai Khan, who held China and all the neighbouring countries in thrall, decided to invade Japan. He began to build ships "in such great numbers," the Chinese poets of the period write, "that the mountains were in mourning for their ravaged forests." Kublai Khan's fleet must have totalled about 3,500 vessels, in which 100,000 warriors embarked.

Learning of this threat, the Japanese prepared to resist the landing. While the non-combatant population assembled in the temples to pray, the Samurai, donning their armour and taking up their swords, bows and arrows, advanced towards the shore to meet the enemy.

At this moment a typhoon of unprecedented violence appeared off the Japanese coast, dispersing and engulfing Kublai Khan's ships. This was the 14th August, 1281. Only a few Mongols escaped and these only landed on Japanese soil to become slaves. The sky, by an obvious intervention, had saved the Empire. "Fall to your knees and render homage to the divine wind of Ise which has destroyed the Tartar fleet," wrote the Emperor Komei.

When the Japanese High Command during the Second World War decided to call for airmen who would voluntarily sacrifice their lives by hurling themselves with their bomb on the target, it gave this special corps the name of "Kamikaze" which means "the Divine Wind" because it was hoped that these volunteers for death would succeed in destroying the American fleet just as the providential typhoon had destroyed its Tartar predecessor.

But contrary to the belief of many people, the decision to create and organize this special corps was not taken at one blow. It did not automatically occur to the Japanese leaders as an obvious application of the national code of chivalry, Bushido, in which suicide after reflection, accomplished according to precise rites (*seppuku*, more often known in the west under the name of *hara-kiri*) is a highly honourable action, obligatory in certain cases.

A study of this question has made me think that Bushido was an archaic feudal monument which should not be quoted in a narrow sense in order to understand the behaviour of the Japanese in a modern war. For example, the code of chivalry attributes the greatest value to respect for the given word and to intransigent loyalty even towards the enemy. We are perfectly well aware that these principles, which applied during small feudal wars, were deliberately rejected by the governments and staffs of all the belligerent countries without exception during the modern wars.

Before thinking of using pilots who would deliberately sacrifice their lives, the Japanese High Command conceived an idea which they called the "Red Operation." These were to be raids where the airmen dropped their bombs normally but from which there was no possibility of return. An aircraft with a range of 2,000 miles would be sent to attack a target situated precisely 2,000 miles away. The radius of action of these aircraft was therefore automatically doubled. The aircraft was sacrificed but the crew were not necessarily sacrificed. They had every chance of saving their lives if not their liberty.

The first Red Operation was a rather unimportant one organized at the beginning of February, 1944. It was directed against the American naval forces moored in the lagoon of the Majuro atoll in the Marshall Islands.

The Captain Mitsuo Fuchido* wrote in an article published after the war: "Had we possessed about thirty elite pilots we should have been able to carry out our plan." The elite Japanese pilots who had been chosen, taught and trained for weeks, had nearly all been killed during the naval air battles in the Coral Sea (May, 1942) and at Midway (June, 1942). The loss of pilots had taken place too swiftly to allow the perfection of this formation.

In short, the Red Operation planned against Majuro probably comprised less than thirty aircraft and left no trace in American naval archives for the very good reason that it never took place: on the morning of the day fixed for the attack the American Fleet left Majuro to bomb the Truk atoll in the Carolines. Then it sailed for the Marianas, after this for the Palaus, and finally for the Philippines. The Japanese Air Command had been taken off its guard by the speed of the American tide.

It is probable that the inventor of the real suicide attack in which the pilot flung himself directly on his target was

* Former member of the staff of the Combined Squadron, then of Supreme Headquarters, Mitsuo Fuchida took part in the attack on Pearl Harbour, as leader of the first wave of assault aircraft. He survived the war and is now mainly busied in agriculture in the Nara district near the temple of Kashihara.

Captain Jyo, commander of the aircraft carrier *Chiyoda*. In any case, it was he who officially proposed the adoption of this method to the Commander-in-Chief of the Combined Squadron.

"I request the honour of being the first pilot to use it." he added.

"If such a method could bring us certain victory," replied the Commander-in-Chief, after thinking the matter over, "we would give orders to all our pilots, down to the last, to use it. But we have only the results to consider."

This meant that the proposal was rejected.

A little later this same proposal was made to surpreme headquarters by a famous fighter pilot, Captain Okamura. This one called the suicide pilot corps "the swarm of bees" because bees die once they have stung. His proposal, like that of Jyo, was rejected.

In the meantime the American offensive gathered strength in the whole Pacific. The Japanese Supreme Command then reversed its decision. Units of suicide pilots were formed and given the name of Kamikazes. At the beginning of this chapter I have described the first attack made by these Kamikazes led by Lieutenant Yuhiho Seki, against the American escort carriers on the 25th October, 1944, in the Gulf of Leyte.

The first Kamikazes flew and died in Zeros carrying a 500 lb. bomb in their belly. But now that the idea had been accepted and put into practice, the means for perfecting the tactics were considered in order to render the sacrifice of these volunteers for death more effective.

"We must carry out these attacks on targets situated beyond the Zeros' radius of action," said one of them. "We should use Shikki Rikko twin-engined bombers which have a larger range."

"We have not enough of these twin-engined aircraft to sacrifice them in Kamikaze attacks," replied the Admiral who had been approached.

"According to my plan they will not be sacrificed. Each of them will carry to the vicinity of the target the machine destined to be sacrificed with its pilot. It will be carried under the fuselage and will be released at the moment of the attack."

"The Shikki Rikko cannot carry a fighter or any other aircraft beneath its fuselage," replied the Admiral.

"Here is the plan of a machine which could be carried in this way."

The machine in question was a guided flying bomb, about fifteen feet long with a pointed nose containing a charge of 2,000 lb. of explosive, a cockpit with elementary controls, a twin rudder and four tubes for jet propulsion. There was room for a man in these flying bombs which, once dropped from the mother bomber, could fly for a few minutes at 550 m.p.h.

The Japanese named the flying bombs carried by the bombers "Maru Dai." When the Americans had a chance to examine one they called it by the Japanese word baka which means mad. The Kamikaze Zeros and the bakas were employed concurrently until the end.

A Kamikaze-baka group was formed at Kanoya, the air base of Kyushu, the southernmost of the islands forming the Japanese mainland. It was under the command of Lieutenant Kuromaru, an excellent pilot who had survived the battles of the Coral Sea and Midway. On the 9th March, 1945, at midday, Kuromaru received orders to attack with his group that evening an American task force, anchored in the lagoon of Ulithi Atoll in the Mariana Islands.

The airmen who were to pilot these flying bombs – like the Zero Kamikazes – were chosen from the countless volunteers who had presented themselves to serve in this special corps as soon as its creation had been officially announced.

The volunteers came from the Army and the Navy as well as from the Air Force. They were not all accepted, for the High Command preferred to keep experienced pilots for non-Kamikaze missions: missions, in fact, from which they could return. Those accepted received privileges and special honours which enhanced the status of their family. While they were alive they were national heroes. Their technical training was extremely simple since their mission consisted of diving on the target as soon as it came in sight, until they crashed.

The Kanoye air base was situated at the foot of three very outstanding mountains in the flanks of which shelters for aircraft had been dug. On the 9th March, 1945, towards twilight, the mechanics dragged the aircraft out of these tunnels while the pilots advanced with great solemnity over the runway. They were all Kamikazes, for the orders envisaged that if the target were to be discovered too late for the flying bomb to be dropped, the twin engines themselves would hurtle down, keeping the bomb attached to their fuselage.

The airmen all wore the ceremonial tunic with black buttons, adorned with the special emblem of the corps – a cherry blossom with three leaves. Each of them also wore round his neck a silk muffler on which was painted traditional poems, often extracts from the works of Norinaga Motoori. "If you are questioned on the subject of the state of mind of a true Japanese, draw a blossom of wild cherry, gleaming in the sun." Or again, "The cherry blossom is the king of flowers. Just as the warrior is the king of men."

Once the aircraft had been lined up on the runway, the base Commandant saluted the *morituri*, waving the national emblem of the Rising Sun. The airmen replied by unfurling their scarves and waving in return. "Even the coldest hearted men could not witness this scene without weeping," wrote Mitsuo Fuchida. At that moment an officer ran up and said a few words to the Base Commandant. The latter went to Kuromaru's aircraft and a few seconds later the Lieutenant, leader of the operation, got out of his plane. The attack was delayed by twenty-four hours.

According to the code of Bushido, the sacrifice of one's life, in order to have some significance, must not be accomplished under pressure of violent despair or in the throes of excitement, in which case it is only a brutal action without moral value and even dishonourable. It must be thought out deliberately in advance and accepted in cold blood. Mitsuo Fuchido does not conceal, however, that the postponement by twenty-four hours of the operation against Ulithi was a terrible ordeal for the Kamikazes. "The combatants were discouraged. There is a limit to the strength of inner will-power. The will to die cannot be acquired by impulsive strength." The total application of the principles of Bushido in modern warfare did not always transpire without difficulty.

On the following day, however, the same airmen, still determined to sacrifice their lives, marched once more across the airfield and the ceremony took place again. This time the departure order was given. The aircraft flew off over the mountains.

Kuromaru's formation had about 1,200 miles to cover in a south-westerly direction. They were to reach Ulithi just at nightfall. At this hour the attackers would be less visible and less vulnerable than in a full daylight attack; the enemy warships would still appear as dark outlines on the sea.

Kuromaru was disappointed, on calculating his bearings, to find that the distance covered did not correspond to the forecasts. He realized that the violent wind which was blowing from the south-east had slowed down their progress although the engines were giving their maximum revs.

An hour later this naval lieutenant took another bearing and felt his spirits sink. Impeded by the head wind, the formation was advancing even more slowly. It was now certain that they would never reach Ulithi before nightfall. The High Command had not allowed a sufficiently wide margin of time. The sun had set and already the surface of the sea was dark. What was to be done?

The idea of giving the order to turn about was unthinkable. The Kamikazes had already postponed their sacrifice by twenty-four hours and Kuromaru knew by his own experience what this effort had cost in nervous energy. Could one possibly exact this effort a second time?

Navigation by the stars does not allow an aircraft at night to locate a target with absolute precision, particularly when a violent wind is blowing. Even in the event of the formation reaching Ulithi and spotting the atoll, or rather guessing its location, the American warships would certainly be blacked-out and invisible.

The only reasonable solution was to postpone the attack until the following day and turn back. However, Lieutenant Kuromaru could not make up his mind to give this order. The men under his command and he himself had already been living too long in a world where rational solutions no longer held good.

The sea below was now completely black and only the upper parts of the sky were still faintly lit. The formation was still flying south-east. Kuromaru obstinately scanned the dark face of the ocean in the hope that perhaps he had been mistaken in his calculations: that Ulithi was not as far away as he had reckoned or that perhaps the enemy warships would appear and that it would still be possible to distinguish and attack them. But no, nothing but darkness which grew ever more dense. ... The operation was a failure. Lieutenant Kuromaru made up his mind. He gave the order over the radio and turned back with his aircraft. As he examined the sky, which was a little less dark than the sea, he saw that the other machines were following him and carrying out the same manoeuvre.

One of the bombers did not follow him. Did the pilot fail to receive the order or did he deliberately disobey? No one has ever known. Of the bombers who turned back with their *bakas* under the fuselage some did not get back to Kanoya from lack of fuel. Kuromaru himself had to land in the sea but he was picked up. Only later did he learn that one aircraft of his group had continued to fly south-east in the pitch darkness and had spotted the target.

On the evening of the 10th March, 1945, the Ulithi atoll looked almost as though it were peace-time. The swift tropical twilight had given place to a starry night. The chiefs of the American Armada, which for months had gone from victory to victory, felt so strong and safe that the ships anchored in this lagoon so far from any enemy base only observed a token blackout. Through the chinks of the big 'tween-decks of the carriers and on the deck of various other vessels could be seen the bright patches of cinema screens. The crews were relaxing in perfect comfort before setting sail on new forays.

Suddenly the voices of the characters in a gangster film being shown on the aircraft carrier *Randolph* were drowned by a gigantic explosion. All the men leapt up. On the screen the images imperturbably continued their now ridiculous dialogue. Klaxons sounded and everyone ran to his action station.

A fire was burning on the flying deck and other explosions could be heard to stern. The general opinion was that an American fighter in trouble had just clumsily crashed on the *Randolph*. Only on the following day when they examined the burnt-out debris of the aircraft on the stern of the carrier (it suffered only superficial damage) did the Americans realize that it was Japanese.

The war now became more and more grim for Japan. On the 10th March, Tokyo had its twelfth bombing attack. Three hundred Super Fortresses from Guam dropped 1,200 tons of bombs on the city "I have never seen such an impressive sight as that of Tokyo in flames," declared General Thomas Power when he got out of his aircraft. "More than twenty-five square miles of the capital has been destroyed."

"In February and March, 1945, I was at Totori air base near Kyoto," Second Lieutenant Tabuchi the observer told me. "We suffered ever more severe bombings and one of them was carried out by 1,700 aircraft. In our shelters we saw the American bombers fly in at low altitudes between the mountains and up the length of our valley, dropping their loads. Our anti-aircraft was useless for lack of ammunition." This survivor told me his tragic memories with a smile and offered me a cigarette. On the walls of his room I was able to admire canvasses and very beautiful drawings of French romanesque sculpture. From time to time we stopped discussing the war to look at reproductions of Japanese sculpture, certain of which had an almost Greek beauty. Outside huge trees swayed gently in the sunlight. Rarely had the horrors of war been so remote. . . .

Before attacking the great island of Okinawa, 500 miles south of Tokyo and 350 miles from Nagasaki – 120 miles long, very outstanding and with a varying width of three to fifteen miles in places – the Americans decided to capture the islands, or rather the Kerama islets which lie in a chain ten to forty-five miles west of the southernmost point of Okinawa. The archipelago was defended by a garrison of about 800 men. No aircraft. The conquest posed no difficulties.

The Americans were inclined to be benevolent towards the natives who had survived the preliminary bombardment, but the latter gave them an idea of what a landing on Japanese soil could be like before unconditional surrender. They died in their hundreds. The Americans discovered, mingled with the corpses of the adults, those of children killed by their parents in collective suicide. On the 1st April, 1945, when the first assault waves of marines landed on the north shore of Okinawa, which had been pulverized by the air force and the naval guns and transformed into a positively lunar landscape, they did not find a single Japanese. The whole of the day's advance (cautious, for a preceding conquest, that of Iwojima, had taught them a great deal about the science and defensive determination of the Nippon warriors) they did not see a trace of an enemy. It was only on the 5th April that the American troops who had continued their march to the south at last made contact and found grim evidence of the Japanese command to abandon the north part of the island and to concentrate the whole of the garrison (about 60,000 men) and the population (200,000 inhabitants) in the south. Every male civilian from sixteen to sixty had been issued with weapons so as to form a redoubt capable of holding up the American advance for several weeks: during this time the main objective was to *destroy the American warships*, the continual presence of which was absolutely essential to the landed troops, by massive Kamikaze attacks.

Although the *baka* method had never been abandoned, the Japanese command employed more and more simple Kamikazes, flying single-seater aircraft and crashing with their 500 lb. bomb, for the American advance made targets more and more easy to reach.

"At that time I was at the air base at Kisarazu, near Tokyo," the ex-observer officer, Tabuchi said to me. "On the 4th April, I took off in my Saiun aircraft, which flew at nearly 400 miles an hour and could take 1,250 photos with its automatic camera. I flew over the American fleet at Okinawa and returned with my photographs."

"Weren't you engaged by the ack-ack over Okinawa,

or attacked by American fighters?"

"No, I flew and took my photos at 30,000 feet. I only saw one American fighter on the trip, but he did not see me. The photos were needed to prepare for the great Kamikaze operation. They were enlarged and the staff officers examined the importance of the American task force."

These officers could report that 1,400 vessels had assembled in the waters of Okinawa. Under magnification they identified the heavy aircraft carriers, the light carriers, the battleships and the cruisers. The Kamikazes were to dive on these big units. A single one of these suicide pilots on his own could either sink a big ship or at least damage it sufficiently to put it out of action.

Left on their own, the destroyers, the transports and landing craft would fall an easy prey to the Japanese squadron, the remains of the Imperial Fleet which had been assembled into a final squadron. The latter, one must not forget, would include the battleship *Yamato*, the famous 63,000-ton giant with nine 16-inch guns. Why should they not still hope? If the Americans had to give up Okinawa and saw their fleet seriously diminished they might well abandon the idea of conquering Japan and finally propose an honourable peace, the Japanese reasoned. This time it was truly the fate of the Empire which the volunteers for death held in their hands. They would be the divine wind itself, or else no more Japanese would exist on the devastated island.

The targets were allocated and orders dispatched to the airfields of Kyushu and the Ryuku islands. The largest part of the normal aviation had been transferred to the central islands of Japan which they were to defend, but the Kamikaze formation had remained on the advance airfield. These volunteers for death should have the shortest route to cover to attack the American ships, for the training of their pilots had been never more speedy and summary.

To be accurate, their volunteering was now quite relative: young people found themselves appointed as Kamikazes. They were chosen in particular from among students of literature and law, their comrades from the science faculties having already all been drafted into the factories as technicians. A certain number of these designated volunteers refused to join the special corps. They preferred to commit suicide.

"Was it because they were afraid?" I asked ex-Second Lieutenant Kabuchi.

"No, since they killed themselves. They merely exercised their right as human beings. According to the Japanese code of morality this right merely allowed them to kill themselves and not to prefer life to death."

The first great Kamikaze attack against the American fleet assembled off Okinawa took place on the 6th April, 1945. The aircraft flown were old Zeros, dive-bombers of the 1937 vintage, torpedo-carrying aircraft and out-dated seaplanes. Among these volunteers for death were a certain number of fast twin-engine bombers and new Zeros flown by experienced pilots destined to guide the flock to their objectives: four or five hundred aircraft in all.

From dawn the sky, which had been alternately bright and cloudy on the preceding days, was now completely overcast. The wind blew from the north at 8 to 10 m.p.h. The ceremonial of the departure does not seem to have been rigorously adhered to because of the American bombing attacks. The formations took off in the rain on runways dotted with water-logged bomb craters. There were several accidents at take-off and aircraft were seen to burst into flames and explode before leaving the soil. For those pilots the sacrifice had already been accomplished. The others flew off in the direction of Okinawa, led by their shepherds.

The grey sea lay below the swarms of aircraft. The pilots stared at the horizon, waiting to see loom up ahead of them the mountain mass of Okinawa, the last land they would see before dying. Perhaps in their imagination they saw once more the places where they had spent their life, their town or their village, the little carefully-cultivated fields, some loved face – or perhaps they were only thinking of the glorious beyond which their sacrifice would allow them to penetrate in a moment. For all occidentals, even for those who have lived a long time in Japan, the secrets of the Japanese soul have remained a mystery.

Okinawa duly loomed on the horizon in the dawn when the first groups of enemy fighters appeared. The American radar operators had seen the enemy formations on their screens and the aircraft had taken off from the carriers. They were Grumman F.6.F Hellcats equipped with a 2,000 h.p. engine capable of reaching a speed of 500 m.p.h. and armed with six 50 mm. cannon firing automatically from the wings. The American pilots were a chosen body of robust, magnificently trained men with a very high morale. They had learned their fighting experience in the course of several difficult but victorious battles.

They flashed like wolves among the flock of Kamikazes and caused a terrible carnage. The suicide squad continued to fly on without even putting up a defence, straight towards the first ships they could now make out on the ocean.

These ships were destroyers equipped as radar picket ships; in other words, provided with long-distance equipment to identify aircraft. The Americans had placed them in a circle north-west of Okinawa and these vessels bore the brunt of the Kamikaze attack.

Many of the pilots hurled themselves on the first ship they saw. Without doubt their inner tension was too great to allow them to wait any longer. Others, however, pressed on and made for the bigger units.

About half the effectives of this attack were intercepted and shot down by the fighters. The figures of the Japanese air losses of the 6th April, printed in various documents, do not agree. The highest is 561 and the lowest 307. The figure of American losses: two aircraft!

A second mass attack took place on the following day, the 7th April. As previously, the Kamikazes were encircled by non-suicide aircraft, in all about 180 machines. 58 were shot down by the carrier fighters and 35 by anti-aircraft from the warships.

American documents do not give the number of Kamikazes who managed to reach their targets and of course the Japanese never knew. "The percentage of hits was very small," one reads in an American report. "Nevertheless one has the impression that if they went on the effect of these attacks would be catastrophic for us."

Were the Kamikazes going to succeeded in saving the Empire? On the Japanese side they began to doubt it. Numerous American warships had been destroyed but not the most important, and that very 7th April the last Imperial Squadron composed of the *Yamato*, a cruiser and eight destroyers, received the *coup-de-grâce*.

The High Command had sent it to sea in the hope that it would find the American fleet dismembered by the Kamikaze attacks. Instead of this it was attacked to the north-west of Okinawa by aircraft of a task force sent out specially to meet it. Wave after wave of dive-bombers and torpedo-carrying aircraft hurtled down on the *Yamato*. The colossal floating fortress sailed majestically, surmounted by a multi-coloured plume of fire from its ack-ack. But this defence was not sufficient and nothing could replace the sunk Japanese aircraft carriers. The *Yamato* succumbed. Its 63,000-ton mass finally exploded in an enormous orange glow without leaving a single survivor on the surface of the sea. The cruiser and the five destroyers were also sunk. The Imperial Fleet had ceased to exist and with it the hope of destroying the American warships which had survived the Kamikaze attacks.

Nevertheless, the Japanese Command organized several more attacks during the Okinawa campaign, which lasted until the 21st June. They took place at intervals of seven to ten days. In all, 35 American ships were sunk, including thirteen destroyers and 22 smaller craft. 299 units were damaged. Out of the ten heavy aircraft carriers engaged, eight were ultimately damaged to varying degrees. These results which the Americans found impressive – they did not hide the fact – did not force them to raise the seige of Okinawa.

Each wave of suicide aircraft which took off from the bombed airfields set out with less hope than the one preceding. The airmen knew that the fiery circle was drawing closer round their country and that their sacrifice would hardly suffice to spare them the humiliation of seeing the sacred soil of Japan desecrated by the presence of white barbarians.

In addition, the difference between the Kamikaze attacks

and the normal attacks tended to disappear. Many pilots who did not belong to the special corps now voluntarily crashed with their bombs on their targets. The survivors of the last Japanese air squadrons seemed to have adopted as their device, *All of us are Kamikazes.*

But the word Kamikaze now rang like a note of despair.

With the conquest of Okinawa, the Americans installed an air base there. Every day thousands of Super Fortresses took off from Okinawa, Iwojima and Sipam to plaster the harbours, the industrial centres and the cities. The last vestiges of the Imperial Fleet were destroyed at Kure and Yokosaka. The Japanese Air Force, bombed and machine-gunned daily on its airfields, reduced to a few squadrons, deprived of fuel and ammunition, could no longer react.

We know that the last episode of this tragedy was the almost total destruction of two Japanese cities by the atomic bomb. On the 7th August, the President of the United States of America warned the Japanese that they could expect a rain of ruin such as had never been witnessed before on earth. On the 8th August, the U.S.S.R. declared war on Japan. The Mikado's Government capitulated on the 15th August.

The last act of the tragedy had been played but it was said that the Kamikazes would appear once more on the stage before the curtain fell, as though to give the world a truly Japanese epilogue. On the 16th August the Chief of Staff of the 5th Air Squadron took off at the head of thirty aircraft and every one of them crashed on the American base of Okinawa. Another formation of the same squadron took the air and set out in the direction of the sea. While the aircraft were flying above the immensity of the ocean one of them dived straight down into the water. In strict order, each of its comrades followed suit. There was not a single survivor. The Kamikazes had made their last gesture.

ALL QUIET ON THE WESTERN FRONT 5/-

Erich Maria Remarque

Erich Maria Remarque belongs to a family of
French extraction that emigrated into
Germany at the time of the French Revolution
and settled in the Rhineland. In 1914 at the
age of 18 he went straight from school into the
army and was sent to the Western Front.
During the course of the war his mother died
and all his friends were killed. At the end of
the war he found himself alone in the world.
He wrote his book, without taking previous
thought, about his own and his friends'
experiences in the war. It arose out of the
consideration that so many men of his
generation, who were yet still young,
nevertheless lived a friendless, embittered,
resigned life without knowing why.
All Quiet on the Western Front
sets out to describe three things: the war, the
fate of a generation and true comradeship.